MW00998905

The SELLING of the SOVIET EMPIRE

Politics & Economics
of Russia's Privatization—

Revelations of the Principal Insider

by

ALFRED KOKH, Ph.D.

LIBERTY
PUBLISHING
HOUSE

Translated from the Russian Text entitled:

PRIVATIZATSIYA V ROSSII
EKONOMIKA I POLITIKA
ALFRED KOKH

Project Editor: Ilya I. Levkov
Liberty Publishing House

For further information, contact:
S.P.I. Books
136 West 22nd Street
New York, NY 10011
Tel: 212/633-2023
Fax: 212/633-2123

9 8 7 6 5 4 3 2
First Edition

Library of Congress Cataloging-in-Publication Data available.
S.P.I. Books World Wide Web address: spibooks.com
ISBN: 1-56171-984-6

Editor of the American Edition Samuel Bartos

"Judge not that ye be not judged."
—*Matthew 7:1*

To Yury Skuratov, Prosecutor General of Russia, without whose intervention this book would only have been received as an economics treatise!

ACKNOWLEDGMENT

This book is the result of the challenging work done by my dedicated professional colleagues and myself during the period of 1992 through 1997.

I would like especially to thank Anatoly Chubais, Petr Mostovoy, and Dimitry Vassiliyev, who were the original initiators of the process of privatization in Russia. I would also like to acknowledge the endless love and devotion of my wife, Marina, during this difficult period of our lives.

May, 1998

Alfred Kokh
New York

CONTENTS

FOREWORD 11

INTRODUCTION 24

───────────────────────────────────── CHAPTER I

THE VOUCHER STAGE OF PRIVATIZATION 29

    Anatoly Sobchak 32

    Lenin at the Smolny 35

    The Vouchers Arrive 36

───────────────────────────────────── CHAPTER II

THE EARLY MONETARY PERIOD OF

    PRIVATIZATION 43

    Monetary Strategy 45

    Small-Scale Privatization 48

Sale of Shares 50

Structural Reforms 53

The Development of a Stock Market 56

Voucher Investment Funds 57

Investments 58

Foreign Investments:

Russia's Émigrés Come Home 60

Birds of a Feather 62

Back to Square One 63

Beyond Good and Evil 65

The Equity Market Crisis:

    The Last Quarter of 1994 67

The Krasnoyarsk Aluminum Plant 68

Polevanism 73

A Fly in the Ointment 79

The Bright Future 84

=== CHAPTER III

THE SECOND STAGE OF MONETARY

    PRIVATIZATION: 1995 87

Privatization after the Expiration of the

Vouchers: Objectives for 1995 90

Sales Strategy in 1995 99

=== CHAPTER IV

THE PLEDGE PLAN 103

General Description 110

Our Errors 113

Norilsky Nickel 115

YUKOS 123

Sibneft 126

Convertible Bonds 131

Svyazinvest 1995 133

National and Regional

    Specialized Auctions 135

Financial Results of 1995 143

Quantitative Results of 1995 145

Advantages of Private Property 146

Bankruptcy or Not 148

=== CHAPTER V

SAME STRATEGY, NEW TACTICS: 1996 150

    Alexander Kazakov, Master of Defense 156

    The State Audit Office vs. Kokh

        and Mostovoy 158

    The Fifth Chairman of the State

        Property Committee 161

    Privatization Has a Fiscal Nature 162

    Improving Both the Quality of Management

        and the Efficient Use of Federal Property 163

    Management of State Property 164

    A New Stage in the Management

        of StateProperty 171

    Privatization Strategy in 1996 176

    For New Times, a New Privatization

        Program: 1996 186

    Results of Conversion of State Enterprises

        into Joint-Stock Companies 188

    Strategies for Deploying Privatization

        Methods 190

    Financial Results of 1996 191

    The Privatization of Real Estate 194

Creation of the Register of State
   Property Assets 195
Dividends on Shares in Federal Ownership 197
Comparative Analysis of the Performance
   of State-Owned and Privatized Companies 198

=== CHAPTER VI
THE HOT SUMMER OF 1997 201
   The Duma's Favorite Bete Noire 203
   The Tyumen Oil Company 206
   Svyazinvest 1997 210
   Norilsky Nickel 213

CONCLUSION 217

Tables 221
Personalities 228
Author's Biography 233
Index 235

FOREWORD

To the Reader:

No book can keep up with the pace of current events in the Russian Federation. Hence, this author has had to write yet another foreword to help you understand the book and the political context of its genesis. It will also provide an idea of events that have unfolded since it was written. For example, while the book was being readied for publication, the so-called War of the Oligarchs (also called the Bankers' War) escalated, resulting in a profound political crisis and the outright dismissal of the Government in March of 1998. As I am writing this in late March, the Chernomyrdin Government has been forced to resign and Sergey Kiriyenko, a 35-year-old until recently Fuel and Energy Minister, has been entrusted with forming a new cabinet.

I suppose what the readers expect from me is sensational reports from the battlefield of this Bankers' War and the truth about its main protagonists. This is a fair presumption; so let me try to outline what—to my mind—was driving this war and what led to its results. (On the other hand, I am not sure about the permanence of these results: the hostilities may break out again, in a different form and over new spoils.)

A package of stock in Rosneft, one the last State-owned oil companies, was recently put up for auction. The opening price of the 75%+1 share package came to $2.1 billion, according to the estimate made by Dresdner Kleinwort Benson. I do not think there is a link between the announcement of the auction and the sacking of the government at the same time. The way the auction is being configured, no banking group stands to gain from it directly; they admit that the starting price of $2.1 billion is very high. Any talk about this kind of price benefiting anyone is at least foolish. When the dust settles, it will become clear who the benefactor is; but for now such conclusions are premature. On the other hand, I suspect that, should the auction take place and the warring groups fail to come up with the funds, there may be new emotional outbursts and new battles in the media wars.

So: the Bankers' War. According to some, it was brought about by the auction at which 25% of Svyazinvest stock was sold. I disagree: I think that auction was the last straw, exhausting the patience of the largest banking groups, in particular those headed by Vladimir Gusinsky, Boris Berezovsky, Mikhail Khodorkovsky and MENATEP/YUKOS, and maybe also SBS-Agro. They felt that the results of the auction left them squeezed out, for up until the last moment they believed that privatized major Russian companies would be "divvied up" on "fair" terms, rather than simply going to the highest bidder. Perhaps it is our fault, and the fault of the Government, that we failed to communicate to them that for a number of objective reasons there would be no "fair" terms, nor can there be. The main reason is that, given the situation, this "divvying up" is simply not, nor will it ever be, in the interest of the Government. In the spring and summer of 1997 the proceeds from privatization were a vital source of budgetary income, needed for solving a number of problems outlined by the President, first and foremost of which being back pay owed to budgetary personnel and the military. We needed to sell Svyazinvest as badly as we had needed to sell any number of other privatized items, for as much as we could.

Some will say that all other auctions had been conducted in the "divvying-up" fashion. This is really not quite true: if we examine the large auctions held before and after Svyazinvest, we will see only two forms in which they were held:

One form was the sale held on the basis of a pledge auction arranged by creditor banks, in which case the Government had very little say. In particular, the May 1997 auction of the 51% stock package of Sibneft was held by the Oil Financing Company (NFK), which was holding the pledge. The Government could not influence the way it was held: whatever happened, happened. Of course, not everyone was happy, and as far as I know litigation continues. Nonetheless, as early as 1995, the Government offered assurances to the effect that these auctions would be entrusted to the party that had pledged the stock. The same thing happened in the case of Norilsky Nickel.

For this reason, I consider the criticism of these two auctions groundless. Any criticism concerning a lack of openness in these auctions is in fact criticism of pledge auctions as such. At the same time, neither warring side has ever criticized pledge auctions; on the contrary, they have considered these auctions a positive development. I share this opinion.

As for other 1997 auctions—Svyazinvest, Eastern Oil Company (VNK), and Tyumen Oil Company (TNK)—contrary to media allegations, the Government never extended any preferential treatment to any banks or promised to put them in charge of these auctions. The only objective in these auctions was to get the best prices for the stock being sold. (An example of an excellent auction was the December 1997 specialized large sale of shares of Eastern Oil Company. The winner, the Rosprom-YUKOS group, ended up paying over 5 trillion rubles for 42% of the stock, which was the maximum amount we could get.)

All of this makes the accusations regarding the Svyazinvest auction absurd: one might as well criticize us for the VNK and TNK and any other auction. Not one of them involved any "divvying up." Nor could there have been such a deal: it was not what the Government wanted. Besides, we needed the money badly for the budget.

The Svyazinvest charges persist, though I do not quite understand why: I categorically reject the charge that we strengthened the UNEXIM bank group by "passing" them Svyazinvest. The winner paid a real price, and the losing party came in with a lower bid. In fact, no one made any procedural complaints.

Another popular gambit is that auctions of such huge chunks of State property shouldn't be based on the principle of maximum stock prices. These accusers claim that there is a certain banking community, ruled by a certain multiparty insider agreement, and that tilting the balance toward one of these parties—even though they have the funds—will have an adverse effect on the competition; hence, that in such situations the Government must be concerned not merely with its income but with structural issues as well, specifically that the acquisition of Svyazinvest made the UNEXIM group unduly strong. Supposedly the sale should have been arranged in such a way that the package went to the other consortium, which of course now claims to believe it has been cheated.

I see a certain element of hypocrisy there. For the sake of argument, let us allow that, indeed, high stock prices should not be the only criterion. Then where were these critics when the MENATEP group, acting through YUKOS, acquired a controlling share in VNK? If UNEXIM had made the same purchase, there would have been an outburst about its growth. Yet the acquisition of VNK strengthened MENATEP substantially, especially after YUKOS and Sibneft merged into the YUKSI company a few months ago. In fact, the birth of this oil giant was acclaimed by the media.

Finally, another argument, never voiced explicitly, but always lingering: Certain parties, in particular the MOST bank and the group controlled by Boris Berezovsky, were very helpful to Yeltsin in the 1996 election and felt they were owed a reimbursement of sorts—specifically, Svyazinvest. When they didn't get it, they felt they had been cheated and launched the media campaign. I do not believe that this kind of arrangement is justified at all.

"Gentlemen!" I would say to them. "If you indeed fought against Russian Communism and for the Russian capitalism that we have created through our joint efforts, then you were fighting over your own money, which, if the Communist candidate Gennady Zyuganov had won, would have turned to dust. This is the real reason you support Yeltsin—not because you were expecting compensation! First and foremost, you were protecting yourselves, your business, and your lives—and only then Yeltsin and his Government."

(Incidentally, Gazprom, which contributed to the campaign as much as anyone else, never asked for any compensation.)

It's also no secret that Mr. Berezovsky was allowed to acquire ORT (Russian public TV) through his people so that he could help the President win the election. That isn't adequate compensation?

In sum, I find all these explanations of the roots of the Bankers' War offered by our opponents unconvincing. In my mind, there is only one reason, and it is quite simple:

Imagine a group of businessmen, all in the same position, with comparable amounts of capital. Bang! goes the starting pistol, and they race off into the brave new world of privatization. Some businessmen begin buying up factories, investing in the industrial sector. Others prefer to channel their money into creating media empires that will monopolize the airwaves, thus forming public opinion, and force the Government to extend them special protection. Now, should the government fail to do so, its most "disobedient" representatives will have to be vilified in the media. Then, wielding this "media cudgel," these businessmen will start investing in other areas at reduced costs, or else they will start acquiring control of industries, not through buying companies or their stock but by forcing appointments of their own people to the various boards.

I believe that the Government committed a grave error by overlooking the danger of this media monopoly and continuing to imagine that our media are diverse enough to give an objective picture of the Russian economy and politics. After this monopoly took shape, a real force was generated that is capable of provoking national political crises and forcing the Government to either take certain actions or resign.

This is how the summer of 1997 came to be. Then we were faced with an explicit ultimatum: "Either the UNEXIM bank is barred from the Svyazinvest auction or we start a media campaign, which we will win, because we have the means to do so and you don't. We form public opinion, we shape the situation, we toss in the compromising evidence, we influence the electorate and the Duma and provoke a crisis." In my opinion, the

Government acted absolutely correctly by not acceding to this blackmail, and now we are dealing with the consequences.

On the other hand, it is this rejection that allowed us to conduct the Eastern Oil Company auction in a normal mode, i.e., with no one voicing surprise at the rules put in effect. Further, this made it possible to conduct the Rosneft auction in an absolutely open, uncompromising fashion. What happened, happened. Once again, I must emphasize that the Government had no alternative: giving in to the blackmail would have whetted the media moguls' appetites further. A surrender would have led them to think that

a) their investment policies had been correct;
b) manipulating the government through the media is an effective way of seizing more and more industries; and
c) those who had invested in industrial production had been wrong.

I do not think that we have yet arrived at a fundamental comprehension of Russia's latest political crisis. I also do not believe that we are sturdy enough to resist this sort of blackmail in the future. Yet I am convinced that, should the media monopoly be allowed to remain unbroken, political crises in Russia will recur with the regularity and predictability of a Swiss watch movement. The Government could, of course, just stop selling off property and quit privatization altogether. This I find unacceptable: as I have said repeatedly, the State is the most inefficient proprietor; this has been proven by many studies, and the Western reader hardly needs more arguments.

Another important feature of the latest Russian crisis that is worth stressing is a lack of cohesion in our political establishment. Somehow a number of our leading politicians, including ministers, have decided to ensure longer political lives by

17

veering from one group to another. Perhaps unwillingly, former Minister of the Interior Anatoly Kulikov actively weighed in on the side of banking and media moguls, who, I understand, promised him certain favors, such as keeping his media image untainted, etc. Then, as a result of the same moguls' efforts, he lost his job. Perhaps it would have been easier if he had joined in with the rest of the Government; this would have helped us conduct our policy more relentlessly and proved to the oligarchs the impossibility of compromise based on media blackmail.

Kulikov's case is a good lesson for the new cabinet, soon to be nominated. They will understand that a policy of compromise with this sort of people is impossible, not because they're inherently vicious or diabolically inclined. Compromise with media moguls is impossible because, as I have already said, their investment strategy presupposes obtaining substantial economic favors by creating media pressure on the government. If this pressure fails to achieve its objective and yields the moguls no favors, then the money invested in creating their empires will have been wasted. The moguls cannot allow that to happen, for it will lead to their bankruptcy. They have invested in a tool that does not work. Now they feel they simply have to make it work, and the only way to do it is to provoke a political crisis entailing the dismissal of the entire Government. Which is exactly what happened in March of 1998.

That dismissal was a logical outcome of the political crisis that followed the settlement of the Svyazinvest account. A Government is designed to govern a country, insofar as it is possible, under a market-economy system. A complex country like Russia can be governed only by a team that acts with concerted effort. As soon as it fails to do so, it stops performing its function and becomes useless. I do not believe in coalition Governments in general: they are possible in states where the role of the Government is minimal and where the economy is governed by the market's invisible hand regardless of the Government. Only in such a situation is a compromise solution like coalition government feasible, and even then it remains practically unworkable. There are plenty of examples. One is Italy, where cabinets change in the twinkling of an eye. At the same time, there is never a coalition in the United States, nor in England, where the Government is formed by the ruling party; nor, for all practical purposes, in Germany, where even with their parliamentary system it is hard to imagine a Government that would include both Christian Democrats and Social Democrats.

Surely, coalition government cannot function in a transition-stage economy that requires serious reforms which must be implemented by a strong executive authority. This is the reason we reject coalition government for Russia. The only choice is a Government that works as one team. This is the only kind that can effect reform. When in March 1997 President Yeltsin formed a Government that included myself and (more importantly) Anatoly Chubais and Boris Nemtsov, we worked as one team until the summer, or until the Svyazinvest auction. We set down well-formulated objectives, and we reached them: we paid the pensions, the Army salaries, and, finally, by January 1998, all the budget workers' salaries.

Once the media started putting pressure on the Government, once some of its members were compromised while others were flirted with, the Government as a team ceased to exist. The President was justified in saying that the Government was no longer performing its work: it was no longer effecting the reform, working for economic growth, etc. The first time Yeltsin said it in January, then he repeated it in February, and in March he gave up, saying: If you keep fighting, if you distrust one another, if you're no longer a team—you're dismissed. And the first one to go was the Prime Minister, who had let things slide to the point where, instead of one team, he had two warring groups: Anatoly Kulikov's and Anatoly Chubais's.

It was clear that these groups represented two different policies. Chubais and his supporters, the so-called young reformers, realize that the solution to Russia's problems lies down the path of structural reform: We must change the form of property and the configuration of large corporations; we must demonopolize the latter; and we must liberalize prices, especially in housing. Whereas Kulikov's group believes that we do not need radical changes, that these change are harmful and lead to further criminalization of society; that privatization of the economy leads to a high crime rate; and that the only way to put the country in order is to go back to centralized control of the economy. Kulikov's prescription for the economy is well-known, mostly through his own speeches—nationalization of banks and large corporations, etc.

As I mentioned, Sergey Kiriyenko has been entrusted with forming a new cabinet. I believe that if the media pressure on the government comes to a stop, that cabinet will be able to work as a team. If not, we will see disintegration and chaos once again. Therefore, in order to protect itself from another dismissal, the Government must make the demonopolization of the media its first priority.

Let's call a spade a spade. Evidently, 70% of the Russian media are controlled by Boris Berezovsky and Vladimir Gusinsky. Print media have substantially less effect on public opinion than radio and TV; I am speaking primarily of TV channels. Of the three national channels, two—One (ORT) and Four (NTV)—belong to these two gentlemen. Gusinsky owns NTV outright. As for ORT, the State holds the controlling share, but informally it belongs to Berezovsky. It is easy to imagine what one can do with such enormous potential. The State-owned Russian Channel is too weak to compete with the others' news departments. This is why I maintain that these two control 70% of the media. Which is not to say that people are incapable of forming their own ideas. But no one in the Russian political establishment—no decision maker, as opposed to a mere observer—no such person can withstand the pressure of these groups. Immediately, they will concoct a cartoonish image of a bribe-taker, a skirt-chaser, a Public Enemy Number One. In today's world you can't have a long political life with this kind of image, not if you want to stay on top of the Mount Olympus of Russian politics.

It seems to me that Russia is facing a choice. One option is putting up with the media dictatorship, proving indirectly that the moguls' investment strategy was right and that they can blackmail the Government endlessly. I consider this a dead-end strategy, since it could lead to intense political instability and all-out confrontation, a civil war, and a total about-face of the political course. From what I understand, this is not an outcome the moguls want either.

The other option is for the Government to break up the monopoly, though not necessarily by expropriation. There are several ways to do this, primarily by creating opportunities for other media empires to emerge; only this will lead to the diversity of opinion we need. One could bring this about by opening up new frequencies, new channels that would serve as the basis for new TV companies, new newspapers, radio stations, and so forth. We must review radically our licensing policy; that is, the policy of the Communications Ministry in the area of the airwaves. Also, we must make the State property work for the State—by which

I mean most of all the currently "dormant" controlling share of ORT, but also refer to the idea of privatizing Channel Two. Such a policy would provide alternatives to the current media groups; together they could deliver an objective picture of the situation in the country, rather than one needed by a particular group of two or three people. Or the Government should find the money to bolster the State-owned Russian Channel and enable it to provide ORT and NTV with real competition, escaping from the bottom of the ratings list. I do not see any other alternatives for the Government.

Summing up the preliminary results of the Bankers' War—or, rather, the political crisis termed so by the media—I would have to say that it ended in a draw. Neither side has gained an obvious advantage, and the only substantial—and harmful—upshot is further political instability, which has been made worse by a financial crisis and has led to the stagnation of the stock market and of investment in Russia. The main task of the new Government is to return political stability to the level of the summer of 1997, and move back to investment-based economic growth.

In general, analyzing the situation in the spring of 1998, I find reason for cautious optimism. In Russia, we do not have objective grounds for an economic crisis. We have weathered the financial crisis in Southwest Asia; now, once we get rid of political instability, we have no alternative but economic growth. This is what makes me an optimist for the immediate future, regarding both the Duma election in December 1999 and the Presidential one of 2000.

Alfred Kokh
Moscow, March 1998

Postscript:

As this book was going to press, new Russian government financial and political crises took place demonstrating the political reversibility of Russian politics. As I had indicated on page 17 of the Forward.

"I do not think that we have arrived at a fundamental comprehension of Russia's political crisis. I also do not believe that we are sturdy enough to resist this sort of blackmail in the future."

Indeed, three major events took place this week:

1. The Russian government allowed a defacto devaluation of the ruble, reversing its position on the subject.
2. President Yeltsin decided to appease Russia's banks and the Communist members of the Duma by firing the reform government headed by S. Kiriyenko and reappointing Chernomyrdin and then Y. Primakov.
3. Foreseeing the potential pressure from the left and searching for reassurance from the government to honor repayment of bonds the government had issued, the leading banks decided to boldly merge. Thus the previous state of relations that was characterized as "Bankers Wars" can now be referred to as "Bankers Peace."

These developments signify that the financial reforms we had initiated are being slowed down. I do sincerely hope that it is only a temporary maneuver of the president rather than a drastic change in the course of Russia's economic and financial reforms.

Alfred Kokh
September 10, 1998

INTRODUCTION

Russian privatization was really a huge, risky, and unique experiment. A way had to be found to convert an immense dinosaur, the centrally planned Marxist economy, into a flexible modern-day capitalist one. Nothing like it had ever been tried on such a vast scale—let alone accomplished.

O f course a certain kind of privatization had been going on for years during the Gorbachev era—spontaneously, microscopically, legally, as the mom-and-pop sidewalk concerns of everyday life were allowed to be *de facto* privatized, that is, taken over by the individuals who were running them. Everyone had some idea of what it was to own a couple of goats or a baker's oven—so the concept was not exactly 100% foreign. But beyond those two goats the concept of property was very vague, weak, even feared and despised; we knew that after leaning on the State for direction for decades, the Russian people could only with painful missteps learn to own and run their own rich country.

What made the challenge so intense was the gigantism of those decades—the bankrupt philosophy that bigger is better. We were forced to deal with a Soviet economy that by this time consisted mainly of mammoth State enterprises. Now figuring out how to convert your corner grocery store into a private concern might not be rocket science, but how was an enormous industrial complex like Uralmash—whose list of products reads like an encyclopedia of heavy industry—going to be turned into a newly private company?

This was a country whose citizenry couldn't tell a stock from a bond and was basically unable to imagine any form of property but State ownership. Russian companies had always been State-owned, so that for the Russian people, accepting our efforts to privatize the economy was a frightening leap into the unknown.

Privatization was officially born on July 3, 1991, when the Duma, the freshly redesigned Parliament of the Russian Federation, passed a new law entitled "On the Privatization of State and Municipal Enterprises in the Russian Republic."

The implementation of this project is generally associated with the name of Yegor Gaidar (acting Prime Minister in 1991 and 1992) and his team. But it had actually already taken form earlier, during the time I was working in Leningrad as the head of the city's privatization project in 1991. In those days, my old professor and friend Vitaly Naishul and I used to get together in Repino, a suburb of St. Petersburg, and brainstorm over a glass or two of vodka about what the best way to transfer State businesses to the private sector would be. I initially proposed that we distribute all property for free: we could create a special organization that would sign over State property to the citizens of the country—whether they wanted it or not! The chaos and bewilderment that could well have resulted from such a radical oversimplification was averted when Naishul came up with a far better idea: distributing vouchers, the holders of which could then easily choose to invest them wherever they liked. Such certificates could be retainable, tradable, and accountable.

With this inspired idea my shy, pure-hearted academic friend had invented a formula that would be used to call into being a vast, complex system—out of nothing at all!

The responsibility for implementing the voucher idea was Anatoly Chubais's; he is another wonderful though very different figure, the hardest-working person I have ever known. After the voucher period, however, when the handling of actual money in huge quantities had to be understood and implemented, I was appointed to the leadership position. As the controversies and battles about privatization raged, Professor Naishul almost disavowed his own invention. By that time, Parliament had passed the illiberal Nominal Privatization Act, which among other things did not allow the private trading of stock. Soon thereafter, however, it was Chubais, the Chairman of the State Committee for Privatization, who proposed that we abandon the existing system altogether and issue "bearer" vouchers that could be bought and sold. A fierce fight ensued in the Supreme Soviet (this was still under the old Constitution), but we managed to push this controversial voucher concept through.

Who opposed us and fought so fiercely against vouchers? There were really two groups. The hard-line Communists were of course ideologically totally opposed to any privatization. The second group—the main one opposing vouchers—were younger Communists who believed there should be severe restrictions prohibiting vouchers from being resold, traded, or exchanged. They wanted vouchers restricted to the purchase of partial ownership in soon-to-be privatized companies—for voucher holders to be able to use them only in the acquisition of future stock offerings. This would effectively prevent the accumulation of vouchers in the hands of persons or institutions that might then be able to take majority control over a forthcoming privatized company.

Here's how our voucher system was going to work: In 1992, each of Russia's approximately 150 million citizens—every man, woman, and child—would receive one voucher. Each voucher had a value of 10,000 rubles (around 100 U.S. dollars at the time). Even newborn babies would get them as long as they were born before September 1, 1992. (By chance, it happened that my younger daughter Olga was born just after the deadline, missing it by a mere matter of hours. Without my knowledge, Chubais, my boss and the head of the privatization process, briefly withdrew the voucher eligibility proposal and then resubmitted it to President Boris Yeltsin bearing the revised date of September 2, 1992. Yeltsin signed it, having no idea why Chubais had wanted to adjust the date. And so my new daughter—not to mention all the other babies born that night—also became eligible for a voucher, thanks to this rather creative act of personal kindness on the part of my boss.)

In the end, Professor Naishul did not care much for what his original idea turned into, but I, along with many others, decided it would be best to go forward with what we had. Voucher privatization was conducted under the direct leadership of

Anatoly Chubais, and I was only one of the organizers; therefore, I will deal only briefly with this subject. But I was directly responsible for the development and implementation of the post-voucher phase of privatization that began after July 1, 1994, and this process I will describe in depth.

This book is first and foremost about our privatization team, the group of professionals imported from St. Petersburg by Anatoly Chubais. It included distinguished experts like Dmitry Vassilyev (now Chairman of the Russian equivalent of the Securities and Exchange Commission in the U.S.), Sergey Ignatiyev (now the First Deputy Minister of Finance), and Sergey Vassiliyev (Russia's equivalent of the director of the U.S. Government's General Accounting Office), in addition to myself.

Economists and journalists in Russia and abroad have tended to portray the history of privatization in neatly divided stages. Others simply single out two periods: the voucher period and the monetary period. My experience in dealing with the actual history indicated that it was less clear-cut—that it was really an integral, continuous process; and at times it was the same process simply acquiring a different shape. For example, we started by selling shares for vouchers, then moved on to selling them for cash. As privatization gathered momentum, popular attitudes also changed. Back in 1992, for example, we were seriously debating whether commerce ought to be privatized. In today's Russia, by contrast, even the Communists have joined in supporting the concept of a mixed economy, part State-owned, part private.

By the time you, the reader, have finished this book, you too will understand this dramatic story.

CHAPTER I

THE VOUCHER STAGE
OF PRIVATIZATION

I n analyzing the Russian process of privatization, certain basic factors should be kept in mind. Among the most obvious are the conditions that prevailed in the country as we prepared to meet the challenge, like the fact that large elements of the population had at this point no means of subsistence, while others had been growing very rich very fast; this was only one of various forms of glaring social inequality typical of our society. We also realized that something had to be done about the total lack of foreign investment, before conditions would improve.

Against such a setting, a phenomenon like "spontaneous privatizations" was perhaps to be expected: incredible cases of managements declaring unilaterally that their own companies, up until then the property of the Russian Government, were now the property of a select management team. From late 1988 through July of 1991, thousands of State-owned companies large and small—from two to three percent of all companies that would ultimately be privatized in Russia—were converted in this frightening way en masse into other forms of ownership, lacking any legally established framework. Billions of dollars' worth of Sate assets were literally stolen this way by management teams brazen enough to risk the consequences in the hazy legal vacuum of the period.

Many of these rogue companies eventually went out of business; their managers had never had to turn a profit under the old system, and most of them had been only marginally capable of running a company. They now found themselves unable to keep pace and compete with the new streamlined, nimble entities we helped to create. More government property was stolen every day; our team was under tremendous pressure to come up quickly with a workable, legal method of privatizing the economy.

And we knew that the step-by-step kind of privatization that had been going on in other countries would not be up to the job. The example of Margaret Thatcher's England, where very effective privatizations of individual enterprises had been carried out one by one, involving careful analyses of their specific financial structures, strengths, and needs—British Gas, the Postal Service, their telecommunications companies come to mind—would not help us now. Such tailor-made, piecemeal privatizations wouldn't change the very structure of ownership in our country, which was what we had to do.

What we needed was a simple, understandable, standardized method of total privatization, a magic formula (or so it seemed as we tried to dream it up) that would quickly and rationally turn nearly the entire economy over into private hands. How could we find a way to do so much so quickly? Perhaps it was a case of necessity being the mother of invention, for the enemies of democracy and of the free market—especially the Communists who wanted to turn the clock back—would have liked nothing better than to see us fail to turn the Russian economic dinosaur into a modern economic system—and then get rid of us and all of the others working hard for reform and democracy.

But we succeeded: In the 1992–94 period alone we privatized more than 240,000 enterprises. And the instrument we invented to work this miracle was the voucher—officially known as the "Privatization Check." Distribution of vouchers to the Russian people began on October 1, 1992; this was during my tenure as Deputy Chairman of the St. Petersburg Committee for State Property Management, or KUGI, of which Sergey Belyaev was Chairman. (It was also during my time at this job that the name of the city changed from Leningrad to St. Petersburg.)

And then, in 1993, the State Property Committee itself—the Moscow privatization team headed by Anatoly Chubais—found itself pressed for time and lacking manpower; so they invited me to come to Moscow to help them complete voucher privatization... In fact, I left St. Petersburg without regrets, as it was by then clear to me that I had not endeared myself to Mayor Anatoly Sobchak.

ANATOLY SOBCHAK

The mayor of St. Petersburg did not view Chubais's privatization team with favor; in fact he took every opportunity to dissociate himself from it. As a matter of fact, Chubais had been a member of the St. Petersburg city Government once; immediately upon assuming office, however, Sobchak had removed Chubais as First Deputy Chairman of the (then) Leningrad Executive Committee and had made him his "economics counselor"—without, by the way, any specific powers—and Director of the Leontieff Center, an economics think tank founded in association with Nobel Prize-winner Wassily Leontieff. With these hollow appointments Sobchak had rendered Chubais a powerless figurehead, and as far as I know never again asked his advice—whether Chubais was in St. Petersburg or Moscow.

This was partly because the mayor was not as strong on economics as he might have been. Yes, he had been a university law professor, but mainly he was one of these politicians whose grand self-image is his principal asset. The meaning of what we were trying to do with the economy and for the population of average Russians clearly took a back seat to personal political advantage. No, it was the "city fathers"—the managers of the factories and the large department stores—that Sobchak was courting and catering to. Whenever our efforts led to a clash with these wheelers and dealers, you could be sure what side he'd be on. He would profess to see no value in our privatization activities, and as he was reluctant to criticize Sergey Belyaev, his own personal appointee, his resentment, his disdain for the privatization process would be diverted to me, as I occupied the "hot seat" and was directly in charge of privatization at the Committee for State Property Management. Sobchak was not going to fire me—he understood he would have problems with Moscow if he tried—but he turned the heat on, criticizing me publicly at every opportunity.

In those days St. Petersburg's esteemed mayor was in the habit of speaking out of two sides of his mouth: whenever he was away from his dukedom on the Neva traveling in the West, he drank in the praise he received everywhere for how well privatization was proceeding in his city. He bragged about the great results that had been achieved, and was repeatedly hailed as a great reformer. As soon as he arrived home in St. Petersburg, however, this old Communist would pack up the export rhetoric and roll out the domestic version: just the approach of your basic production guy who understood tube assortments, 6x9 mandrels, and other heavy-industry trivia, but on whom the long-term significance of what we were trying to achieve with privatization was completely lost.

I remember one time when we were starting to privatize the prominent Dieta (dietetic food store) on St. Petersburg's main street, Nevsky Prospekt. Its manager, an influential woman who had long played a role providing the city's power brokers with hard-to-find imported foodstuffs, started making a lot of noise as soon as we started privatizing her establishment like any other store. A virtual scandal erupted, flurries of letters were coming in, Sobchak's wife, Lyudmila Narussova, got involved, all of it singling me out as a villain who would turn a neighborhood store into a large commercial one with exorbitant prices and let poor sick people be left without their dietetic food. I was a menace to society! On one of his letters, Sobchak scribbled the words "Attn. Belyaev: Bring Kokh to his senses, or else I'll do it myself!—Sobchak."

But neither Belyaev nor Sobchak ever succeeded in "bringing me to my senses" (not that Belyaev, to the best of my knowledge, ever wanted to), and today that privatized store is over-flowing with ten times as much dietetic food as it ever carried in the past—and at competetive prices.

Ironically enough, Sobchak found himself with no support when he tried to mount a reelection campaign. Even First Deputy Prime Minister Oleg Soskovets, whom Sobchak had regularly praised in the media and elsewhere, deserted him, joining with Alexandr Korzhakov, head of the presidential security apparatus (equivalent to the U.S. Secret Service), and Mikhail Barsukov (head of the KGB) to pick Vladimir Yakovlev, the popular and effective head of the committee that managed city property and infrastructure in St. Petersburg, to succeed Sobchak.

Of course, by this time in our history we chose our mayors in real elections, they were not imposed on us by such eminen-cies; but that particular election was very, very close (Yakovlev won by half a percent). It happens to be the case that these powerful gentlemen did use their influence—by leaking damag-ing or scandalous information to the press, some of it about an apartment that Sobchak had obtained in not quite the right way. It is clear that their disfavor was crucial.

The fact is that Anatoly Sobchak never had any compre-hensible, clearly defined economic objectives. He would claim to be a solid democrat and reformer, but constantly changed positions as he switched from one group of economists to another, in effect doing his best to sabotage any real headway that was being made. Oddly enough, it was Chubais and his team that supported him more than anyone else, for which he showed no appreciation. He failed to make himself politically attractive to us or even to other solid hands-on managers like himself—even these natural allies were never able to accept him on their terms.

Speaking of such personalities and the way they affect people's lives reminds me of the personality we Russians, in a way, knew best and of the day in 1992 when we literally walked in his footsteps, to make a very important point.

This was really the most, well, cinematic moment I personally experienced, in the exciting story of Russia's privatization.

LENIN AT THE SMOLNY

When one thinks of this era in our country's history, among the most vivid images that come to mind are the Lenin icons—portraits, statues, the shrine on Red Square—so many of which were toppled from their honored spots at this time.

We felt it was our turn to contribute our own historic version to this process.

The scene I would like to tell you about was based on one that used to be drummed into the head of every Russian boy and girl:

It's the middle of the night in St. Petersburg, the birthplace of the Bolshevik Revolution, November 7, 1917 (commemorated ever after as the most sacred day of the Soviet year). The Winter Palace has been stormed and occupied by the Red Guards and there's an all-night session in the main hall of the Smolny Institute, a meeting of representatives of the *soviets*—the new grass-roots legislative councils—from all across the country. Lenin ascends the podium and proclaims to the packed house—arm outstretched, cap in hand—the success of the proletarian revolution, uttering the famous phrase, "ALL POWER TO THE SOVIETS!!!"

This had been for us the principal image of the Russian Revolution, endlessly immortalized.

And so in 1992 we decided that our historic event would symbolically take place in the same hall—it was still there, in the Smolny—in this treasured hall, before the fifteen-foot-high portrait of Lenin, still in the same pose, that had always hung just where that podium had stood. We assembled all the directors and managers of all those mammoth State enterprises, and I stood before them, right in front of the portrait, and proclaimed, "THIS IS THE MOMENT WHEN WE BEGIN THE PRIVATIZATION OF RUSSIA. LENIN HAS BEEN DISMISSED!!!"

It is perhaps important to note that this new chapter in Russia's history was being written by the thirty-something generation (I, at the time, was just 31). The leading reformers in Moscow in those days were Chubais and Gaidar; they were in their mid-thirties. Even to this day, revolutionary economic reforms continue to be carried out by such thirty-somethings as Sergey Kiriyenko and Boris Nemtsov.

THE VOUCHERS ARRIVE

And now the story of how the new system was born.

Here's how our vouchers worked: Anyone holding one of the vouchers we created could go to the local office of the State Property Fund and choose from a list of upcoming auctions of shares from various companies. Each company would already have been assigned a month when its shares would be auctioned off to voucher holders. Or he could go and deposit it in one of the speculative voucher funds that were soon formed, and wait and see what kind of return the fund's activities would bring him.

36

He could also sell it for money (the original or face value was 10,000 rubles, but vouchers fluctuated in value during their 1992–94 lifetime, reaching as high as 40,000 rubles each). Of course, the typical citizen might have a few vouchers at his disposition, if his wife and children assigned him theirs, which is what typically occurred.

The State Property Fund—if that is where our typical voucher was submitted—would convert it into a share of company stock, with the price determined by a mathematical formula that reflected, among other things, the exact number of shares in that particular company that had been allocated for that particular city. There was a requirement, for example, that if 50 percent of a large factory was being privatized, with 100,000 shares to be auctioned, the event had to be advertised in fifty cities; this was one of the ways the Government was attempting to keep large enterprises from falling into the hands of a relatively small number of voucher holders. Privatization auctions of medium-size factories had to be announced in twenty cities; for small local enterprises, the requirement dropped to one city.

Continuing with our example above, when those 100,000 shares were offered for sale, our typical head-of-household could offer his five or so vouchers to the State Property Fund; after the Fund had sold the shares at the prevailing price it would then also total all the vouchers offered for the shares. To keep things simple, let's assume that 50,000 vouchers had been collected for that particular factory; the number of shares (100,000) would be divided by the quantity of the bid (50,000 vouchers). The resulting valuation would be two shares for every voucher, and Ivan Q. Citizen would become the proud owner of ten shares of that particular widget factory, with each share worth 5,000 rubles.

As the year 1993 drew to a close, the pressure on our office became more and more intense. Privatization by voucher was scheduled to end on January 1, 1994. The deadline had been set by Chubais himself. He had given us 12 months in which to act. We launched more and more companies, trying to give the people opportunities to spend their vouchers. We worked around the clock, with short breaks for sleep, and subsisted on a diet of tea and fast food. But by then we knew that even with our best efforts, only half of the vouchers out there, would be invested by the deadline. Basically, in spite of all that we were doing, there was a frustrating feeling of stasis, of no movement, of deadlock, and we knew that this was because we had not yet been allowed to offer the public the prime companies that represented the real riches of the Russian economy. We also knew that if we failed to get the population to utilize their vouchers (to invest them as described above), things would take a very different turn for the country and for us personally.

So we managed to get the deadline for this mammoth job postponed six months—to June 30, 1994. After all, voucher auctions had only been going on since late 1993, and had been working perfectly throughout Russia. The trouble was, voucher holders were under the impression that nothing would happen if they delayed investing their vouchers, and consequently they were in no hurry. In fact, rather than invest them directly in stocks they had been pooling them in voucher funds, banks, and such, and were turning up their noses at the less than exciting selection of companies that we so far had been able to offer them. And, it must be admitted, they had good reason to be uninspired, since we had been directed to start by auctioning negligible assets. But now, after the extension, in early 1994, we got permission to begin coming up with really attractive offers, including oil companies, large energy concerns like Gazprom, electric power plants, engineering firms, and other heavy-industry companies. And when we did, behold, the vouchers came pouring in, right up until the extended deadline, when we stopped accepting them and those still out there ceased having any value.

And so we found ourselves at the end of voucher privatization, on July 1, 1994, contemplating the fruits of our efforts: over 40 million Russian citizens—30% of the total population—had become owners of shares of privatized enterprises and voucher investment funds. This was a revolutionary achievement: we had created a new social class of property owners, basically by the simple step of giving each citizen of the Russian Federation a voucher representing an equal claim on a portion of State property. According to our information, approximately 98% of all the vouchers had been invested. The balance had now expired and were worthless. We had distributed 151.45 million vouchers, and had collected back 148.58 million through individual purchases of stock. The different categories were as follows: 25.95 million vouchers (17.2% of the total) invested through closed subscriptions, in which particular blocks of stock were allocated by law to the workers in a particular enterprise at a discounted price, 114.69 million (75.7%) through voucher auctions, and 7.9 million (5.2%) by other means such as investment funds. Eighty percent of the investment funds were owned by Russians and 20% were foreign, most of this being German (the Germans were experienced at this game, having gone through privatization in East Germany in 1990–92).

Approximately 116,000 enterprises were privatized, representing about half the economy. This new private sector included over 25,000 stock companies, and was soon producing half of total GDP. Even today, both critics and supporters of voucher privatization agree that in quantitative terms the mass privatization program was an undeniable success. (Probably the only position the two sides have in common.)

We have been blamed for the unfortunate fact that ordinary citizens failed to become Rockefellers. We have been told that we also failed in other ways—that we sold companies too cheaply, that we didn't solicit enough foreign investment, that we missed (unrealistic) deadlines; some of our more emotional opponents—mainly the Communists—never tired of saying this was the Scam of the Century and a scheme for the enrichment of only *nouveau riche* foreigners at the expense of the workers. However, I think we did manage to solve several fundamental problems that had bedeviled the Russian economy. First of all, the State ceased being an inefficient monopolist in the national economy; a sizable number of property owners had now emerged; and the voucher process had given birth to a securities market. When voucher investment funds appeared, so did financial terms like "broker," "registrar," and "trustee." Forty million households had learned the basics of a market economy, thanks to vouchers. This was a guarantee that we would inevitably one day arrive at a well-functioning free-market system. More important, it was a guarantee we would never go back to the dark days of totalitarian state control over the economy.

Admittedly, the game of voucher privatization was not played with perfect rules. If we could go back to 1992 again, we would certainly do things differently. For example: we now realize that we just about destroyed the investment future of many enterprises when we yielded to the populist mood, and allowed closed subscriptions of vouchers, as a "fringe benefit" for employee collectives. All that these disappointed employees gained—after holding onto their stock and digging in their heels, as they tended to do, against the kind of innovations that all of Russia's businesses needed in order to make them viable and to attract investors in the future—were delayed salaries and ridiculously small dividends at the end of the year.

Another blunder we committed was designating many blocks of shares as State property; in some cases, this was due to our hesitance to cause companies to have to sink or swim too suddenly; in other cases, we blocked whole enterprises from being sold because of a whole host of fears that many in and out of government and in the media at the time were expressing—and that we at the time were unfortunately sympathetic toward—about foreigners taking these companies over and closing them down in order to eliminate them as competitors. We were simply afraid of what the new owners might do. But all we accomplished with this kind of conservatism was a situation in which the companies we thought we were protecting suffered even more from lack of new investment.

And when we specifically concentrated on generating new investment, we often failed to get results. At the investment auctions involving the bigger enterprises, we were able to garner the interest of significant investors. Later in the process, where the important thing was future investment, we would allow the stock to be sold to those who would promise to invest the most in the future—and, the truth be told, such promises often tended to remain just that—promises.

Other scenarios also became popular, in some of which the workers were given mostly preferred (nonvoting) stock and management got control; as company operations were renovated blocks of shares that had been held back were sold. The more energetic and creative leadership that began to be exercised as a result of directors and managers of enterprises owning stock was reflected in higher prices at succeeding offerings. But there was always resistance to anything approaching a management buyout, in spite of analogies worldwide, as it was so antithetical to the Russian mentality, which had for so long thought of assets as "common property" and assumed that justice and fairness required the serious participation by the employees in their distribution.

Employee collectives were often thus given powerful privileges unparalleled anywhere else in the world. As it worked out, however, when the employees were not demanding control and then resisting the measures that would make their enterprises more productive and efficient, what they usually did was to buy their stock at the preferential prices they were always offered— and then quickly sell as the market went up. Thus in many companies management was eventually left with a greater stake and more effective control, and found themselves now in a position to innovate and improve the functioning and worth of their enterprises, thereby attracting new investment.

On the whole, voucher privatization was an undeniable success: a private sector and stock market were created; new investment was attracted with newly developed securities; conditions for competition were established; an alternative to the State securities market now existed; and pledge auctions were launched, in which banks loaned the Government money and accepted the new shares as security.

And even in hindsight I cannot join with those who complain that our privatization was too "uncreative," too hasty, too formal or standardized or inflexible. The task was as gigantic as it was worthwhile, and its achievements are really so many that its failings are almost not relevant: without it, the forces favoring capitalism could never have won the presidential elections of 1996, and we would not be seeing equity markets attracting billions of dollars in investments as we are today. Our efforts represented a crucial reinforcement of the country's economic and political reforms, and helped make them irreversible.

CHAPTER II

THE EARLY
MONETARY PERIOD OF
PRIVATIZATION

So the next stage of privatization was announced; during the second half of 1994, laws were passed creating the legal regulatory environment for this stage. We started out with a careful review of the mistakes that had been made in the previous period, in order to correct them to the best of our abilities.

This was to be the "monetary period": voucher investment was over, now we would have outright cash auctions. First, we revised for new offerings the list of privileges to be accorded the employees' collectives, and cut in half the number of enterprises whose shares would be kept out of the sales because they were of either military or strategic importance. And we radically changed our method of fixing starting share prices. Now they would be linked to market quotes, to demand, to the financial situation of the issuer, and to the size of the block issued. We tried hard to revalue previously undervalued shares, hoping that real cash would be attracted to a company whose value was rising—and would thereby also find its way into the State budget.

During the voucher period we had not been as concerned about specific stock prices, since our principal aim was just to inspire the populace to use their vouchers. But in this phase, our goal was to sell the stocks resulting from the voucher process at the highest prices. We had a hard time convincing the market that stocks had been substantially undervalued in the previous period and should be priced much higher than they had been at the initial offering. To take one example: when LUKoil, the largest Russian oil company, was privatized during the voucher period, its share value was approximately one U.S. dollar. As of this writing, it is now valued at more than 2,000% of this amount.

One of my duties was to promote our newly privatized companies in the world at large, both to encourage Western investors and to gain the approval of important players in world finance. On one of the promotional tours we took in this endeavor, for example—this was in late June of 1997—I had the pleasure of meeting with George Soros to discuss the great potential for growth represented by Gazprom, our national gas company, which had recently been privatized.

As I began my presentation, Mr. Soros smiled and gently informed me that his research department had already analyzed the Russian gas and oil industry and that he was already actively involved. We both laughed.

It was a most educational visit, and more than that: as I had caught Mr. Soros in such a good mood, I decided to bring up an important subject that I knew had been under discussion between my staff and the Soros organization for several weeks. Russia was short of cash in June of 1997, and 700 million dollars was needed immediately for pension payments that had been publicly promised by President Yeltsin. The nation's cash problem would only last a few weeks, since a two-billion-dollar Eurobond issue was to mature on July 5. I used this opportunity to gently ask him about a short-term cash loan to alleviate the squeeze that the Russian Federation found itself in and he was most agreeable. The two-week loan's rate was a generously low 9.25%. (By the way, the money loan was from Mr. Soros's personal account, not from one of his investment funds.)

MONETARY STRATEGY We had been working on policies that would be appropriate to the monetary phase of privatization all through the preceding three years. Now we could put them into effect and harvest the fruits of that preparatory work. Many things were going to have to change for the right groundwork of the new system to be properly laid: we would have to radically change our strategy for attracting investment to privatized enterprises; our policies regarding the restructuring of enterprises during privatization would have to change; and old methods of selling securities and real estate would have to be totally revised.

The first stage of privatization had created a new class of property holders, a developing securities market, and had witnessed the emergence of portfolio investors. It was these newly emerging factors that combined to make the second stage of privatization a reality. And that fact is the best proof that our original policies had succeeded—despite all the fierce political opposition that raged against both them and us.

Naturally, there were many compromises along the way, which tainted the final result. For example, a large number of shares remained in the hands of employees; in most of these cases, because they owned so much stock they easily prevented any real restructuring, so nothing was done about the numerous and notorious inefficiencies that had plagued government-owned businesses. Then, toward the end of the formal privatization process, more and more controlling blocks of shares were acquired by the actual professional managers, often because they demanded control in exchange for their help in ensuring worker cooperation in needed changes and in countering the never-ending drumbeat of Communist opposition to reform in the economy. But we knew that the system was still not giving enough voice to the outside shareholders, who as yet did not have the kind of constructive and legitimate input that they have in the West.

Nevertheless, our chosen course made it possible to overcome the major differences between the interests of the State, of the private investors, and of the employees of the companies being privatized. The privatization model we were implementing contained built-in mechanisms aimed at gradual solutions to these problems; chief among these mechanisms was the open buying and selling of joint-stock company shares by shareholders, which became common during privatization. This spurred the development of a securities market in which to trade these shares formally, and led to improvement in the capital structure of the economy. For example, the Russian Trading System, analogous to the Nasdaq market in America, was inaugurated in September 1995. Today, 90% of stocks in Russia are traded using this system.

The new period, which began on July 1, 1994, was totally different from the voucher period. We had been selling off companies really for symbolic prices. Now we were after real prices—prices determined by our companies' true valuations in the open market.

I have always believed that for privatization to succeed in Russia two different approaches would be equally necessary. The social and political dimensions would come first; our first phase had addressed these, creating as it did massive privatization and a powerful private sector, both necessary for a socially oriented market economy.

But now—in 1995—the time had come to turn this into the real thing by concentrating on the economic and financial aspects that were actually just as crucial to our success as social and political factors. We were trying to sell prime companies at top prices; attract investment; maximize revenues from sales; and encourage greater participation from the West—all challenges that are still with us. As we changed our focus, the tempo seemed in fact to slow down, because we were moving from our former forced-march, privatization-for-its-own-sake mode to real, detailed, constructive restructuring and investment. The new model emphasized the continuous formation of new leadership that was responsible and efficient. Two ideas became key: sales were oriented toward investment, and investors could now purchase a controlling block of shares during their primary distribution. Now that the system was functioning and the volume was expanding, I believed it was important that serious investors be inspired to provide investment capital, and so I strongly favored offering them blocks of stock at a discount if they could commit themselves to expanding their involvement in the future, and making sure they had the ability, as they did in the West, to purchase controlling positions in choice companies.

We were concentrating on two types of property: blocks of shares still held by the State in both already privatized companies and companies not as yet released at all from State ownership, and real estate, both State-owned and owned by the newly privatized companies: Because to so many in Russia the private ownership of land was still a bizarre idea, privatized companies up until now had not actually owned the land they stood on, in the sense of having the right to buy and sell it.

As soon as these various projects were set in motion, a renewed flood of income began pouring into State coffers and became available for incorporation into the national budget.

SMALL-SCALE PRIVATIZATION

Let me emphasize for a moment that small-scale privatization, which in a way went back to the Gorbachev era, continued at a fast pace in the monetary period and was a conspicuous success, mainly because of the relative simplicity of running small companies. By early 1995, about 75% of the commercial (i.e., wholesale and retail trading), restaurant, and service sectors had already been privatized.

Our past experiences had demonstrated that auction sales were the most effective way of privatizing enterprises while at the same time avoiding pitfalls like the too rapid and radical conversion of the enterprise, causing an immediate loss of jobs. Many such sales had started taking place in April 1992, in which we sold off company after company at individualized, custom-tailored events designed to raise significant immediate cash; these continued until the advent of voucher privatization at the end of that year.

Vouchers were issued beginning in September of 1992, and by January 1993 they began to be used to acquire actual shares in companies. By 1994, the popularity of auctions had become intense. In over 65% of the small-business sector, the businesses were bought out by their own employees, as follows:

A date and place would be set for all those who wished to bid to show up prepared for the purchase of shares; special advantage was given to the employees if they could represent at least 30% of the company. Such a group would win the auction and would receive a 30% rebate from the State. This was meant both to encourage privatization and a semblance of stability. In some cases a bidding war would erupt between various factions of workers and management; the faction that lost would often leave the company, resulting in a leaner, more dedicated work force.

The years 1992–94 were marked by recession in Russia and a nationwide crisis in which the largest businesses failed to honor their financial obligations or pay salaries. These monstrous problems, reported tirelessly in world media, tended to obscure the quieter forward progress of privatization. But in small businesses, the benefits of privatization were plainly visible to everyone, as the newly privatized enterprises became more nimble in seeking out the resources they needed and in reacting to the consumer market, and as their economic performance began to soar. Suddenly a heretofore unthinkable abundance and broad range of consumer goods began to characterize Russian life, and people discovered that they could finally say good-bye to the very notion of shortages, which had been another notorious and never-ending plague of Soviet life. New owners were suddenly inspired to improve their businesses' appearance and the level of service offered as they experienced natural capitalist impulses to compete for consumers. As if by a miracle, shortages in food, furniture, cars, and clothing all disappeared.

These new owners succeeded in much the same way as the first proprietors of the smallest businesses had, going back to the Gorbachev era. Some of those earlier pioneers had done very well indeed. In fact, many of our offerings found purchasers among the ranks of this newly successful middle class.

According to the State Committee for Statistics, in the first half of 1994 the profitability of private retail businesses—total income divided by profit—amounted to 4.5%. In this period State enterprises were making only 0.5%!

The figures for expenses were 14.6% and 20.9%, respectively; during the period, losses in State-owned enterprises represented 80% of all losses (total losses amounted to 71.5 billion rubles), while the private sector posted a profit of 10.4 billion rubles, or 1.5%.

SALE OF SHARES

The overwhelming majority of large and medium-size enterprises were privatized as open-type joint-stock companies, and their first shares were now issued and sold. ("Open" simply meant that the stock was offered to outsiders; with the "closed" type, stock had to be offered first to insiders, and only after they refused could the stock be offered to the general public.) At this point a total of 33,171 enterprises were listed in the Register of Enterprises; of these, 25,189, or 76%, had already been registered as joint-stock companies. The Committees for the Management of State Property (the equivalent of the Securities and

Exchange Commission in the U.S.) decided to convert 27,512 (83%) of them into joint-stock companies, and privatization plans had been approved for 27,690 (80.5%).

The most active sectors in terms of share issuance in 1994 were the building industry, machinery construction, metal works, transportation, telecommunications, light industry, food, and woodworking.

During the issuance of shares, employee committees over-whelmingly opted for the type of benefits or privileges that allowed them to hold up to 51% of the stock. Such unprecedented privileges made them majority holders of more than 65% of privatized enterprises; such control unfortunately had negative economic consequences, as these worker-owners typically refused to consider the tough changes required to end inefficiencies and begin the massive restructuring that was urgently needed. On the other hand, as I already mentioned, they often soon resold their shares at a profit, relinquishing their negative role.

In 1994, in 72% of all joint-stock companies large investors owned over 10% of the stock; in only 8% did large outside investors own more than 51% of the shares—i.e., a controlling block. Even this early in the privatization process stock was becoming concentrated in the hands of large outside investors and managers whose experience and understanding of the need to operate in a fiscally sound manner enabled them to evaluate the gravity of a company's financial mess faster and more realistically than employees ever could.

Of course, even privatized enterprises had their difficulties. Most of these firms' problems—leaving aside for the moment the question of the nationwide economic recession—were rooted in the inefficiency of new managers and their lack of understanding of the new options available to their companies.

To give an example: under the old system, companies could go to the Government when they needed loans *and they would almost always receive the money*. After the initial privatization period, companies in need of capital could easily offer stock to the market—but few ever pursued this low-cost capital-raising option. Instead they continued in their old ways, taking on more debt from the Government or from banks and paying high interest rates.

Fortunately, there were new managers who knew what they were about, who were adjusting well to the new realities and had the imagination and courage to make real restructuring progress, and they could make quite a contrast with the Communist-era people who had preceded them. In my mind the most striking—comical, perhaps—contrast was displayed by the great nickel-and-platinum mining and refining company Norilsky Nickel.

It seems not to have mattered too much to the old leadership that this company was located beyond the Arctic Circle, so far north in Siberia that no trees grew there. They lured workers to this frigid and barren area with special vacations, summer homes, rest homes, high salaries, bonuses, fresh exotic foods—in short an endless succession of extravagances, considering the location. Some sort of limit or *reductio ad absurdum* was reached when, in their quest for self-sufficiency, they also had the bright idea of setting up furniture factories on the spot, about as far as you could get from any trees, in a place where great sums had to be spent to transport the wood used to make the furniture. Needless to say, this was Russia's most expensive furniture factory! The really serious point—the historic point—is that such irresponsibility used to be common in the U.S.S.R.; it was, in fact, encouraged, since the most unprofitable ventures could endlessly feed on government loans. It is not surprising, then, to find out that virtually all Russian enterprises large and small were heavily in debt.

Now, with the advent of massive privatization, there was new management at Norilsky Nickel. It wasn't long before these "special arrangements," high employee expenditures, unproductive investments, and other wasteful uses of financial resources were swept away. The new managers adopted a simpler and more rational policy, deciding to motivate employees and compensate them for the harsh conditions with higher salaries.

It soon became clear as well that compared with the State sector, the new private sector was both relatively resistant to inflation and efficient in forging new economic relations and developing new markets for its products and services.

STRUCTURAL REFORMS

The earliest years of privatization witnessed important structural reforms in the economy; in the period from 1992 to 1994, over 100 new companies were founded. In the fuel and energy industries, large integrated companies appeared, for whom special organizational regulations had to be developed. The largest Russian gas company, Gazprom, is one example; it was formed by allowing many legally independent companies to unite under one sprawling parent company.

Among the most successful of the large new companies were State holding companies created by the Government in a rational manner, out of the best from among many naturally related entities in such closely related fields as, for example, the extraction, refining, and finishing of the same metals. These became integrated conglomerates; the parent holding company would receive 51% share blocks from these choice subdivisions.

At first the Government would receive and hold on to 100% of the parent company's stock; later, as the new organization gained ground and a reputation, it would sell the shares.

Other successful holding companies were formed through the consolidation of State-owned holdings such as Sovtransavto-holding, which specialized in international freight forwarding, and Aviapribor-holding, which focused on avionics, among other things.

The best-structured transformation was that of the oil industry. In keeping with worldwide practice, the consolidated businesses engaged in the extraction, processing, and sale of crude oil and oil products. Not only did restructuring improve their business flexibility and attract investment, it also led to the formation of a genuinely competitive national market in oil and oil products. These newly privatized entities were soon competitive on the world market as well.

Other examples of the structured transformation of an industry resulted in the formation of the telecommunications companies Rostelekom and Svyazinvest. They turned out so well that they were able to attract foreign investment without compromising national security—despite the fact that they handle Russia's military communications. Rostelekom handles long distance and international calls for all of Russia, while Svyazinvest, which was created from many local telephone companies, provides regional and local service. Since those first years, the two have merged into one conglomerate, Svyazinvest, of which Rostelekom is a division.

In addition to such successes, however, were the duds, State-owned operations joined together for less-than-good reason, that stagnated, failed to grow, and gradually lost their importance as holding companies. These were surpassed by their more nimble competition. For example, when dozens of medium-sized manufacturers of heavy machinery were consolidated to form Rosstanko Instrument, the results were unimpressive and static.

The majority of the holding companies formed by the Government were set up as follows: 49% of the stock would be owned by management, workers and investors; the Government would retain 41% while it waited to see performance and viability, while the holding company itself received only 10%. If they did well, they could buy more of the Government's share. If the results were disappointing the Government would simply liquidate the entire operation, selling its 10%. When things went well, these parent companies often exchanged stock with the individual subsidiaries that were doing well, that is, they would hold the subsidiaries' stock and vice versa. They would often facilitate the arrangement by simply issuing new stock.

Of course, the process of creating holding companies did not always go smoothly. In some instances, the sales of shares were delayed. Partly because the Government itself was confused about the legality of creating these companies, the same enterprise sometimes found itself in two different holding structures. Sometimes even unrelated companies were thoughtlessly bunched into one structure. I remember one of these cases most vividly, when an iron enrichment company, Lebedinsky, was combined with a failing pig farm. It happened simply because the governor of the region wanted to save the farm; as he was a highly influential personality in the area, he could just order the iron works to save it—that is, he went behind the scene and "convinced" the management of Lebedinsky to initiate the combination. Whether you could say everyone was happy I'm not sure, but as a result, the pig farm was able to continue to lose money, the iron-ore company funded the losses, and the governor was happy with his literal "pork."

THE DEVELOPMENT OF A STOCK MARKET

By the end of 1994, there was a real secondary market for new issues of stocks and bonds of privatized businesses. The only larger market was the market for trading State securities and Government treasury bonds. The value of shares issued by newly privatized companies in 1994 exceeded 37 trillion rubles (approximately 7.5 billion in U.S. dollars, based on the exchange rate at the time). Government bonds were traded on an exchange that also traded currency and options. The Moscow Currency Exchange and the secondary market traded on a network called the Russian Trading System (RTS), which is similar to the U.S. Nasdaq system. The most important type of securities circulating in this market was company shares, i.e., securities granting the right to participate in managing a company and to receive dividends based on the company's performance—just like the company shares traded in U.S. markets on U.S. stock exchanges.

The great number of joint-stock companies meant an exponentially increased trading volume in the shares of privatized companies; moderate-to-low starting prices favored rapid growth in value. Those achieving the most accelerated growth in stock prices—outstripping even the explosive pace of inflation during the same period (March 30–September 30, 1994)—were privatized fuel and energy businesses (+1,160%), nonferrous metallurgy (+580%), the construction industry (+550%), and telecommunications (+490%). On a dollar basis, prices of shares of many issuers multiplied 5 to 10 times in 1994.

But this was still definitely only the beginning. There was no question that the Russian market still had considerable potential for growth in share prices. The main condition for this growth, however, was attracting additional investment—especially from abroad.

Internal Russian sources of capital were limited and already exhausted, but that just meant that the market was full of bargains as securities went begging; the explosive growth of the Russian securities market in 1994 was largely due to three billion dollars of foreign portfolio investments, which heated up an already hot emerging market.

All of these developments were leading in one momentous direction: a leap in the capitalization of the entire economy. Beginning in 1991, the valuation of all privatized companies equaled less than 1% of the gross domestic product (GDP); by the end of 1994 it stood at 10% and had left behind all of Eastern Europe, with the exception of the Czech Republic; of course, we still lagged behind most developed capitalist countries.

VOUCHER INVESTMENT FUNDS

One of the sectors of the securities market that saw the most rapid development was the Voucher Investment Funds (VIFs). According to our data, they received one third of all the "privatization checks" issued. During the 1993–94 voucher period, about 650 of these licensed funds were formed, of which 27 had founding capital of more than 10 billion rubles (6 to 7 million U.S. dollars). The greatest number of funds were formed in the Greater Moscow region (200) and in St. Petersburg (47). All were controlled and managed by Russian firms.

The peak period for the VIFs was definitely the first quarter of 1993, when more than half of them were formed. This proliferation fell off in the first half of 1994; their absolute numbers fell by 7% in the second half of that year due to mergers. Their influence was profound in more than one way: since they often ended up with significant stakes in the privatized companies whose stock they bought, they soon made it their business to influence management efficiency and choices regarding foreign and national investors, often by placing their own representatives on boards of directors.

After the end of voucher privatization, the majority of the VIFs intended to retain their status as the rough equivalent of U.S. mutual funds. Sixteen percent were planning to implement secondary issues. However, unlike the case of mutual funds in America, both the VIFs and their shareholders paid tax on the same revenues (the U.S. Government taxes only the fees charged, while gains and income taxes are paid by the shareholder), so it was not long before they generally changed their status from funds to investment companies.

INVESTMENTS Since attracting investment had not been a top priority in the first stage of privatization, investment demand stagnated at that time. In 1993, only 4.3% of the 12,798 auctions were investment-based, i.e., where the purchaser of stock agrees to invest additional money in the company in the future; in 1994, only 4.7% of 5,511 were. But the groundwork of a new system was being laid, and private and commercial investment would soon be strongly attracted to manufacturing industries, thanks to the existence of the new stock market. And as private sources began supplying capital, State funds would be freed and become available for the social sector—housing, schools, child care, etc. In short, by a grand historic irony, the privatization of the economy was going to make it easier, not harder, for the Russian Government to care for its humblest citizens.

But shares of the joint-stock companies created during privatization remained extremely attractive to portfolio investors, and during 1994 the general volume of foreign investment in the stock of Russian privatized businesses amounted to approximately three billion dollars.

At the end of 1994, it was not yet quite clear which Russian industries were sure-fire winners with foreign investors. According to expert estimates, during voucher privatization foreign investors had purchased up to 10% of the shares of privatized enterprises at regular auctions (where the highest bid purchased the stock) and investment-based auctions (where the buyer agreed to invest funds in the company). Most of the interest concentrated on such industries as oil, metallurgy, timber, woodworking, construction materials, food processing, and maritime shipping. Geographically, machinery, food processing, and construction materials had done best in the Moscow region, the chemical industry was associated with the Yaroslavl region, maritime shipping and shipyards reigned in the Arkhangelsk region, while timber loomed large in the Chita region and the Komi Republic.

The main source of capital investment in Russia came from individuals in the United States and Germany who bought through mutual funds in their countries or would do direct deals using investment banking firms. In addition, there were a handful of sophisticated investors who bought directly, such as George Soros, Benjamin Steimatz, and others. Americans invested mainly in the fuel and energy businesses, while Germans invested almost exclusively in chemicals, manufacturing, food processing, and construction materials.

But in spite of how limited foreign investment in privatized companies was, resounding speeches always seemed to be echoing in our ears about national security and about how stock in our national businesses was in danger of being bought up and controlled by foreign investors in order to eliminate competition. The Communists tended to dwell on the lurid theme of Foreign Control; others imagined foreign companies out to destroy their competitors, acquiring and then destroying them. As so very often in the past, Russia was inventing a set of values for itself that few, if any, other countries would bother with. The rest of the world's nations are anxious to draw foreign investment into their economies to help ensure stable economic growth, but this had never interested most Russian politicians, to whom it had never occurred to try and attract foreign investment. I have yet to hear of an emerging economy ever once disdaining foreign capital the way Russia used to.

FOREIGN INVESTMENTS: RUSSIA'S ÉMIGRÉS COME HOME

Whenever we privatization people had an exchange of views with our political opponents concerning the dangers of foreign capital, our strongest argument was always that they could never point to any evidence to support their hysteria. When had any of these terrible things ever happened? As far as I can see, capital is invested in sectors where production is marketed only internally—consumer goods, food industry, retail. Therefore, the objects of investment can't threaten an investor's or his country's interests. Yes, there were small emerging investments in potential export sectors, in three categories: (A) institutional investments by players in the equity market; (B) industrial investments by foreign inves-tors whose profile coincides with that of the recipient; and (C) industrial investments whose aim was to allow the foreign investor to share the capital recipient's profile on the world market.

Some examples from Group A, the institutional investments: Novolipetsk Metallurgy Complex, LOMO (Leningrad Optical and Mechanical Association), Rostelekom, and some mining enterprises: obviously, an institutional investor attracted by growth will not want to push the business he is investing in away from its traditional foreign markets, which could only result in a drop in prices and a profit loss.

Next, Group B, the industrial investments by similar foreign investors: Alfa Laval's investment in the Potok stock company in Kaliningrad, Moscow Region, Schwing-Stetter's investment in the Pushkin Repair and Engineering Works in St. Petersburg, and Salamander's investments in the Russian shoe industry. These investments resulted in the increased export potential of the respective businesses, but almost all these businesses are stable—and were in no way interfered with by their patrons when they appeared on the world market.

Group C, industrial investments by those interested in Russian firms' profiles: Mardima's and Stumhammer's investments in electrical engineering, Trans World Group's investments in metallurgy. Actually, these should not be considered truly foreign, as they are mostly reinvestments by Russian entrepreneurs who had exported their capital and created stable businesses abroad. Mardima (Yekaterinburg) in Germany, the Trans World Group (Moscow) in Great Britain—rather successful small firms created by "overseas Russians" who had emigrated ten or fifteen years before to Israel, the United States, or elsewhere—were now plowing their expertise and money back into Russia.

I honestly don't think we have anything to fear from these former émigré investors. They simply wanted access to markets in Russia that were traditional for the recipients of their investment capital. I have never heard of such investments resulting in substantive negative changes in the Russian business they invested in. If anything, foreign investment capital gave these companies a powerful edge in dealing with their competitors.

Actually, a more relevant point is that these former émigrés were the least efficient type of investors. They had mostly made their capital in trading—buying and selling, import-export. Running such businesses tends to inculcate a certain mindset. People with trading backgrounds have little feel for long-term investment, tend not to be sufficiently trusted by banks, are often lacking in patience, and have had no experience in working with long-term funds and stocks. They rarely have even the modest capital required for major industrial projects, and this just leads to stagnation in the investee and often to an excruciating search for a way out of deals gone bad. Such investors were much like their Russian counterparts, entrepreneurs who founded highly successful firms like Mikrodin and Bioprotsess, chains of consumer-goods stores, with the only differences being their somewhat "foreign" appearance, their exaggerated arrogance, and their ability to take their Russian directors on expensive international junkets.

BIRDS OF A FEATHER Another habitual and pointless misconception that hasn't done us any good, and that we should just get rid of, is the way we love to view Russian industry as the same as that of an economically developed country. For such a long time, we dreamed that we were competing with the United States, Germany, Japan, etc.—countries that had traditionally played the role of investors. In fact, our competitors all during that time were actually Brazil, Mexico, Argentina, China, and the Arab countries. Industrial development in these countries was not too backward, but the most developed sectors were mining and various industries engaged in the first two or three stages of the production process—metallurgy, the manufacture of chemical fertilizers, tree-based industries. These were niches in the world market where we were really competing hard with these other developing countries.

However, in those countries the sectors mentioned belonged either to the State or to native owners, and surplus investment capital was not exactly what characterized their economies, to put it mildly. Their investment potential was comparable to that of Russia, so the last thing they were thinking about was investing in Russia—they had better things to do with their resources. What they were, of course, doing at that time was seeking investments for themselves, and "smart Americans" didn't care whether they invested in Russia or in Mexico. Investments go where the situation is more stable and understandable, where there is less financial and political risk, and where it is less expensive from the point of view of taxation and labor.

Thus I came to the conclusion that foreign investments could not possibly harm Russia's strategic interests. Simply stated, they did not generally come from our main competitors.

BACK TO SQUARE ONE Still, I wanted to bend over backward to be fair and to be sure that I had not ignored any important factors.... I tried to imagine a shrewd and devious foreign investor who secretly wants to ruin a healthy Russian company because it is competing with him on the world market. If we add a reasonable assumption that this investor has no other motivation—geopolitical, patriotic, etc.—than his own profit, what we have is a classical "economic man."

Let us trace the hypothetical stages of implementation that would be required for this sort of project. His initial plan would have to go like this: if the Russian company in question is giving him problems it has to be because its products are either cheaper or of better quality than his own; his aim would be to buy stock to the point of becoming the major shareholder, and then either change the enterprise's profile or close it down altogether.

So he would start buying the shares of his Russian competitor. Eventually, the day would come when the desired objective is reached: the controlling block of shares is in the investor's hands. Notice that this has cost some money: for the shares, for lawyers, brokers, and travel expenses, and for the war of nerves with Russian red tape—but now he controls a company capable of producing a product cheaper and possibly better. Will he change its profile? Why should he, if he can do better with the Russian company than he did with his original one? Will he close it down? That would be stupid! If he sticks to his original strategy of ruining his Russian competitor's company, then instead of obtaining sky-high profits from a newly acquired superior competitor, he will in the end just return to his own less profitable business, and the money spent on purchasing the controlling shares will have produced nothing at all for him.

The intelligent investor would start correcting his initial strategy: He would start investing in the more efficient Russian business (even if it is only potentially more efficient). It is the profile of his own business that he will now try to change: he will reconsider the wisdom of competing against the lower-priced Russian firm and shift his investment to where it will get a better return. Far from closing down his Russian competitor, he will most likely shift some or all of his production in that very direction!

After constructing such a hypothetical case, I inevitably concluded that closing down or changing the profile of a Russian competitor simply does not fit logically with the foreign owner's profit orientation.

BEYOND GOOD AND EVIL I will readily admit that our opponents' fears of ulterior motives and conspiracies were justified insofar as a few selected Russian companies were concerned, those that possessed world-class technologies and whose production was on the highest technical level. The great majority of these belonged to the defense establishment. But even for such companies, the "enemy" would not be a specific firm, whose behavior I believed would always follow the logic I just outlined; no, if there was an enemy to watch out for, it would be a foreign nation with geopolitical ambitions.

Only a state could try to implement such designs, acting through its intelligence services, accumulating budgetary appropriations, and using secret agents and dummy front companies. And such nonsensical designs are admittedly possible anywhere, since a functionary's mentality is always the same: in order to prove that he is needed, he must search for enemies everywhere, whether abroad or in his own backyard. Russians know all about this. What bureaucrat would object to spending secret budgetary appropriations, without controls?

I didn't think that we should base our laws on such far-out, exceptional cases and risk throwing the baby out with the bathwater. By fearing such improbable cases and creating obstacles to accepting foreign investment, we could lose the majority of the investments in our economy as investors shifted to Mexico or other emerging markets. The odd and menacing scenario we are contemplating was getting even more unlikely all the time, as the budgets of foreign intelligence services were being severely cut back at the time. I just didn't think they could sufficiently focus their efforts and resources to cause any substantial damage to any of our privatized companies.

There was one solution: pitch our intelligence services against theirs. This way we could at least find something for our intelligence services to do, which would please a lot of people in our Government.

Incidentally, the first time we did limit the participation of foreign investors in privatization was during the pledge auctions at the end of 1995, a limitation that really only applied to some of the companies being privatized, and that was justified because of their sensitive status. Earlier, we had really had nothing it would have made sense to keep foreigners from bidding on. Investment in the Russian economy was so low, and was perceived to be so risky, that if we had put any limits on, it is highly unlikely that any foreign investors would have gone ahead and started bidding at all. Later, when the situation had radically changed and investment flow into Russia was mounting, we certainly kept the problem vividly in mind, since there were and still are areas of the economy where the penetration of foreign capital would admittedly be undesirable. All countries have to weigh these considerations when it comes to protecting selected industries.

**THE EQUITY
MARKET CRISIS:
THE LAST QUARTER
OF 1994**

Foreign investment reached its peak in August 1994, when it rose to $500 million; by November the demand had dropped to $300 million, in December to $100 million, and in January 1995 to just about $20 million.

By January 1995, foreign orders to buy shares of Russian privatized businesses dropped twenty times.

This collapse of foreign portfolio investments was accompanied by accelerating inflation in October–December 1994, which caused the large majority of personal savings to be channeled into hard currencies (easily purchased from banks) and led to a sharp drop in the share prices of most major issuers. This process continued through December and into January 1995.

There were many reasons for the price drop, but several crucial ones should be stressed. For one thing, the level of shareholder protection in our country was still very low, and this was vividly illustrated by a scandal that erupted at the end of 1994 when several shareholders, Zalogbank in particular, were struck from the shareholders' register of the Krasnoyarsk Aluminum Plant. (A register is the official record of all the owners of the underlying stock in a particular company.) The company responsible for managing the registry acquiesced to a demand from the director of the Krasnoyarsk Aluminum Plant, which owned the registry company (in violation of Russian law), and removed Zalogbank from the list of stockholders, effectively canceling its evidence of ownership. This outrageous and illegal act received worldwide news coverage; in fact, the case is still being litigated. Suffice it to say that international investors were horrified that such behavior could occur in what they had supposed was a well-regulated securities market.

A second reason for the price drop involves the personality of Vladimir Polevanov, who was the new Director of the State Property Committee (GKI) at that time. He was repeatedly quoted as saying that some of the privatization results had to be reviewed, that he even intended to conduct a partial renationalization of some companies. Thirdly, the securities crisis in Mexico had resulted in a sharp drop in institutional investor confidence in all developing markets. The world community had to spend $40 billion to overcome the consequences of the Mexican crisis. Finally, this all happened just at the beginning of the Chechen war.

The first cause mentioned above—the Krasnoyarsk scandal—had long-range consequences for the credibility of the Russian market. The second is extremely revealing about certain sensitive political areas.

THE KRASNOYARSK ALUMINUM PLANT

The conflict at the "Kraz" plant was the prologue to the so-called first aluminum war, and may well stand as the most far-reaching scandal of the privatization era. In the middle of November 1994 the plant administrators crossed Zalogbank (owned by the British Trans World Group) off its stockholders' register. The commercial contract between the plant and the bank ran through the year 2003. The plant management explained its actions by citing a statement of the previous stockholders to the effect that Russky Kapital and Zalogbank had not paid for the shares they had purchased. According to plant representatives, the Trans World Group "violated a whole range of laws related to securities." They cited a faulty written agreement for the purchase of the Kraz stock in which the date of payment for securities was not stipulated; they seized upon this minor omission to declare the contract null and void and thereupon simply "returned the stock to the previous stockholders." Needless to say, the fact that this could happen to an investor in a privatized Russian company caused immediate panic in the market.

This shocking behavior, involving changes being made in the register that damaged stockholders' interests, was possible only because Yury Kolpakov, Kraz's general manager, had had improper direct physical access to the stockholders' register, a total violation of the existing laws—in particular of the President's decree "On Measures to Ensure Stockholder Rights." This decree required that companies with over 1,000 employees transfer their register records to "banks, retailers, depositors, or specialized registrars." The stockholders' register was supposed to be maintained by an independent registrar.

I went personally directly to Krasnoyarsk to investigate this crime, all the way to southern Siberia, close to the Chinese border. As soon as I arrived I began to hear from all sides that in fact no organization in the city existed that could be trusted with a privatized company's stockholders' register.

By now disgusted as well as enraged, I contacted the management there. I realized that the situation could become quite tense and explosive and that dealing directly with the perpetrators in their headquarters could be dangerous. Before leaving for Kraz, I had called the main office of the Federal Security Service (formerly the KGB) and had inquired about my personal safety in this region, asking if they recommended a security detail escort. Within an hour I was called back by the Deputy Director of the

Counterintelligence Division for Industrial Espionage and Security. I was warned to proceed with extreme caution. The situation required immediate investigation, I was told, and a security contingent of their men was deemed necessary. Confirming my darkest fears, I was told that the manager of the factory, Yury Kolpakov, was closely connected with some of the most powerful heads of the criminal underworld, and getting into the factory would take some doing. Unless Kolpakov summoned in an outsider, anyone would be physically barred from entering the factory. I put down the phone glad that I had the wisdom to suspect and fear the substantial power and violence of the Russian "mafia."

I made arrangements to meet my special security detail at the Krasnoyarsk airport. When I got off the plane I was greeted by five heavily armed federal agents packing an assortment of heavy artillery including mini-Kalashnikov machine guns, pistols, and God only knows what else. They were all dressed in menacing black leather coats that covered the weaponry on their persons. Because they were not wearing uniforms, the thought crossed my mind that these guys could be actually part of the local "mafia" coming to kidnap me. They identified themselves and kept me guarded day and night.

My first stop was to the regional governor, Valery Zubov, to explain exactly why I was here. As I sat in front of him, he picked up the phone and called the factory, getting though to Yury Kolpakov as though they were good friends. He explained to Kolpakov that I and some close friends had come from the Government to investigate an irregularity with the stockholders' register. Thanks to this call and the five "close friends" from the security team, I was ushered into the factory without incident, meeting with Kolpakov and simply demanding of him that this inappropriate action be rescinded. There was no reference to illegality or imprisonment; I just told him that the true owner had to be reinstated on the registry, and that if he disputed this in any way it would have to be taken up in the courts.

Despite the heavy aura of genial intimidation, the governor startled me by initially siding with the factory manager and against the Government and the law. On the way to the factory, the governor hinted that Kolpakov and the local organized crime outfit were the law in his neck of the woods. Kolpakov's response was that he did not agree with the Government's position and that the Government could take him to court. Sneering at me, he said, "Who are you that I should listen to anything *you* have to say?"

I looked him in the eye and responded, "I am the Deputy Chairman of the State Committee for the Management of State Property."

The manager simply replied, "This deal has nothing to do with your department. It's a dispute between two private companies."

I told him, "I can see why you think this is a local problem. I have come here to work out this conflict because it has serious ramifications for foreign investors in Russia, and as the person in charge of privatization I left Moscow to effect an immediate solution and prevent any further international damage."

"No," reiterated the manager, as if he hadn't heard me, "it's your problem—take us to court if you don't like it."

"Suit yourself," I sighed, knowing that I didn't yet have the law on my side as effectively as I would have liked—to put it mildly. "I must get back to my work in Moscow."

Unfortunately, given Russia's lack of strong laws to protect investors at this point in 1994, the case dragged on, and this injustice was regrettably not resolved. In light of this case, my associate Dmitry Vassilyev drafted a proposal that was submitted to Parliament and passed into law in 1995. This historic measure was called the "Law for the Regulation of the Stock Market," and provided for extensive new Western-style protections to prevent anything like this from ever happening again.

After my departure, management and supervision of the Krasnoyarsk register were transferred to a firm called Krazbroker. The heads of Trans World Group declared that since 1993 its member firms had acquired 20% of Kraz stock. As is typical of Russian stockholding companies, none of the shareholders, especially the big ones, sought direct profit from possessing their stock. Rather, as strategic investors, their interest in holding stock was determined by a desire to control the enterprise's activities, and in the specific case of Kraz, its trade policy. The block of shares held by the members of Trans World Group had afforded them such a possibility.

Russky Kapital and Zalogbank brought their complaint about the actions of Kraz's director to the Public Prosecutor's regional office, the Russian Fund for Federal Property (RFFI), and four other agencies including the arbitration court. Officially, their claim was listed as: "Protests Against the Krasnoyarsk Aluminum Stock Company's Refusal to Include the Plaintiff in the Stockholders' Register."

Two years of open enmity, litigation, and even (some say) violence ensued before Kraz and the Trans World Group were reconciled enough to cooperate on a project called the Achinsk Alumina Complex, which they intended should reach a production level of 700,000 tons of aluminum by 1997. This joint project was certainly one factor contributing to the end of hostilities; Kraz's desperate financial state and urgent need for a rich partner was another. It should be noted, however, that as of this writing the litigation actually goes on, and there has been no final settlement. (Also the Achinsk project never went anywhere, in fact it went bankrupt. In the end, they were unable to sustain good relations because of the previous enmity and distrust.)

POLEVANISM   "Black Tuesday," in October of 1994, when in one day the ruble fell approximately 20% against the U.S. dollar, led instantly to a Government reshuffling. Viktor Gerashchenko was removed as President of the Central Bank, and Alexandr Shokhin was fired from his job as Deputy Prime Minister in charge of the economy.

Picking a new Deputy Prime Minister responsible for the whole body of economy-related questions was a considerable challenge. True, it could certainly be handled by Anatoly Chubais, partly because he was known and respected in the West as a trusted reformer. He had a solid, reliable reputation and was a credible member of the previous economic reform team headed by Gaidar. Chubais, moreover, was known as a talented executive who had the trust of both the West and of President Boris Yeltsin. But his nomination would inevitably lead to one big problem: who would then succeed him as Chairman of the State Property Committee? At the time none of us—Chubais's deputies—had the necessary political standing and influence to take on this job.

Yeltsin therefore made a political decision: to appeal to the Russian heartland, he nominated Vladimir Polevanov, the governor of the far eastern Amur Region, as Chairman of the State Property Committee and Deputy Prime Minister, even though the man had absolutely no specific economic qualifications for this job (he was originally a geologist by profession).

Later, Chubais admitted that he had proposed Polevanov personally: "For the new problems that the State Property Committee has to solve, we needed a professional like Polevanov." He changed his mind pretty soon, however, and now had to mount a campaign to get the guy fired.

Vladimir Polevanov started his chairmanship, in November 1994, by issuing several remarkable statements. One was to the effect that "hasty privatization of some strategically important industries, in particular aluminum and other defense-related producers, is endangering national security," and he publicly advocated that the Government should consider renationalizing these industries. He declared that privatization had caused $500 million worth of damage to the aluminum industry, claiming, "This money left Russia in the form of exported products of aluminum plants, whose big blocks of shares had been acquired by foreign investors."

For the long term, he proposed to draft a Federal Nationalization Law designed to "strengthen the role of the State" in industries of strategic value to the Russian economy. He ordered a temporary suspension of the sale of shares at cash and investment auctions of aluminum companies like Irkutsk, Bratsk, and Krasnoyarsk, of the Achinsk and Pikalevsk alumina complexes, and of the Western Siberia metallurgy complex.

As the reader may already have figured out, this Polevanov was just echoing the arguments of the Communist opposition. For example, this is the way he described his skepticism toward voucher privatization: "Numerous distortions have caused significant damage to the Russian State system and have weakened national security." Actually, I found a very ironic, almost amusing side to all this: A large part of Polevanov's former job had consisted of privatizing the Amur economy and attracting foreign investors. Now in a spot of high political prominence, he was suddenly mostly concerned with nationalizing industries and chasing away foreign capital!

It was this turnaround in the State Property Committee's policies that was the primary reason for the drop in foreign investments—from $300 million in November 1994 to $20 million in January 1995. According to some estimates, foreign investors who had already bought stock in Russian companies lost around 400% of their money. This was a sharp—and shameful—contrast to the forecasts only recently promulgated by Western financial companies. Later, they estimated that, had it not been for the sudden reversal in the Committee's policy, by spring of 1995 the volume of orders placed by foreign investors to buy stock of Russian companies could have reached $2 to 3 billion per month.

In January 1995, Polevanov sent a "manifesto" to the Prime Minister, demanding that the Government should "immediately abstain from carrying out the second stage of privatization: this stage can be started only after the Russian Parliament adopts a law" suspending trading in the above companies. He also proposed that within the State Property Committee a subcommittee be created in order to "analyze and correct errors committed in the course of privatization of strategically important industries."

Polevanov explained his disagreement with privatization's concepts and results by citing such negative consequences as the growing crime wave (which he felt was due to the redistribution of property), corruption, a criminal housing market made inevitable by the existence of private ownership (if we went back to no one owning anything, he reasoned, no one could be swindled), too much power accumulating in the form of stock in the hands of private persons, as well as damage to Russian national security. He declared, "Privatizations and conversions of State-owned enterprises into joint-stock companies are being carried out with-out taking into account the importance of different sectors and their roles in filling State defense orders."

All this led to an abrupt "cold spell" in the relations between Polevanov and his predecessor. Chubais needed urgently to re-fute Polevanov's statements on possible renationalization. In or-der to calm the hysterical markets and regain the trust of the international investment community, he issued a beautifully simple statement: "Deprivatization in Russia is ruled out." A special an-nouncement by the Russian Government had to be made con-firming the irreversibility of State privatization policies. In particu-lar, the statement said: "All attempts aiming at reconsideration of the privatization results and all calls for nationalization of already privatized enterprises are groundless."

Unfortunately, Polevanov's positions truly represented the very worst nightmares of Western investors regarding the politi-cal risk and instability of doing business in Russia. As a result, Chubais, the founding father of privatization, publicly declared that "Polevanov does not belong in the State Property Commit-tee."

There was one moment that caught Polevanov's essence per-fectly. Once, during a planning meeting, Polevanov started bab-bling again on his favorite topic, how it was necessary to guaran-tee national security while carrying out privatization. It was typical of him that he didn't bother to elaborate on any subject, i.e. actu-ally to discuss mechanisms of protecting national security, to define criteria, or to formulate a specific approach to solving the many problems he was always talking about. He seemed to feel himself above such obligations, and preferred grand "global" dis-cussions, large-scale global thinking about "geopolitical interests," Russia's manifest destiny, and so forth.

After all, before mechanisms for protecting national security can be elaborated, first one has to agree on the terms. I naturally tried to turn the discussion to practical issues. I asked Polevanov if he would first please give us his definition of national security so that we—his deputies—could understand exactly what our boss meant and each of us wouldn't be just acting on the basis of his own understanding of what "security" means. Well, the question stumped Polevanov. It suddenly became apparent to all of us that while he'd been using these bombastic terms, he'd had no idea whatsoever what he was talking about other than on some very general level. He was merely a demagogue spouting rhetoric, hoping to find a constituency among the frustrated Russian population. He had obviously never bothered actually to give these issues any thought that led anywhere, content to simply spout ringing slogans, the way the local church bells in the public squares of little towns in some areas are used to rouse people in an emergency—always sounding the same, whatever the nature of the emergency.

We were all shocked that he couldn't think of an answer. The air was heavy with silence; the situation was getting comical. Finally, Polevanov forced himself to say that he would officially ask the Security Council (headed at the time by Oleg Lobov) to provide him with a definition of national security. As far as I know, he actually made this odd inquiry. Needless to say, he was not taken seriously and there was no answer from the Security Council.

After that, Polevanov bore an active grudge against me. When Prime Minister Viktor Chernomyrdin requested that I go to Kostroma to investigate events described in the media as "nationalization cases," Polevanov overruled him. Well, it was a Government order I didn't feel I could possibly disobey, so I went anyway. Polevanov's reaction was comical. As soon as I got back to Moscow he ordered the guards to keep me out of the building. When I walked through the front door, they asked me for my identification and told me I was not allowed in the building. I asked them if they were prepared to stop me and they replied, "No," so I proceeded to my office and went about my duties.

Petr Mostovoy, another deputy, and I were actually ordered by Polevanov to write letters of resignation. Prime Minister Chernomyrdin refused to sign mine, stating, "I am not satisfied with the reasons you give." In fact, deputies to the Chairman of the State Property Committee were nominated by the Government rather than by the chairman himself, and Polevanov's arbitrary action had raised hackles upstairs. As a result, Mostovoy and I took a brief leave of absence, knowing that Polevanov would soon be fired himself.

That fight completely discredited Polevanov. He became a laughingstock in his own Committee, and it became evident that an amateur like him, with no authority or backing from his superiors, could not last long. He avoided meeting heads of regional committees or making decisions. Shortly before he was dismissed by President Yeltsin in January 1995, something unprecedented took place. At a routine board session of the State Property Committee, Polevanov's position was not supported by a single person. The Chairman ended up being a minority of one.

Contrary to the tenor of the foregoing, I truly do not wish to sit in personal judgment of Polevanov. He has always been, and still remains, a decent human being. But his lack of a basic economic education (his degree was in mineralogy), his lack of vision in the area of economic development, his complete inability to get along with the Moscow powers that be – all of these made him unsuitable for the position of Chairman of the State Property

Committee. Under the circumstances, he ended up indiscriminately criticizing everything and everyone, in the meantime constantly repeating his favorite ringing cliches like "undermining strategic interests" and "nationalization." For all these reasons, he lasted less than two months in the position.

But those two months had had their effect. Between the persistent lack of shareholder protection exemplified by the Krasnoyarsk caper and all this blabbing about dangers to strategic industries and the possibility of renationalization, the sharp collapse of the market was probably inevitable. Such factors could not help but plant serious doubts in the mind of any sane investor of whatever description.

A FLY IN THE OINTMENT

In fact, the period 1992–94 was characterized by a whole range of disappointing or counterproductive aspects of privatization. For one thing, it became evident that the Government's policy of retaining large blocks of privatized company stock was inefficient, due to the fact that in the many, many companies in which the Government still retained a stake it always placed its representatives on the board of directors—and the fact is that these people were generally not capable of running these entities as profitable concerns.

In addition, while the financial results of private companies can in no way be distinguished from those of companies with some stock still in State hands, the latter are unable to attract investment with secondary issues.

It is important to understand that there were three types of privatized companies in Russia: One was sold in toto, 100%, representing total privatization. The second type of sale involved the government selling a 25% plus-one-share block; in the third, the government sold 49% and retained 51%, thus remaining in control. Because the Government was bound by the principle of maintaining its level of control in all these selected companies, if there were to be a secondary issue it would itself have to buy either 25% or 51% of the issue to maintain its level of ownership. Imagine how likely it was for this Government, with its perennial financial problems, to create such obligations for itself, let alone hosts of them. It reminds me of some of the imaginary objects in certain branches of mathematics: it's not going to happen—no secondary issues. Besides the fact that such stock companies under partial Government control had turned out to be clearly unattractive to investors.

And keep in mind certain other persistent factors that we have been well aware of, including the obvious inefficiency of old Soviet methods of managing large enterprises, which emphasized burdening these partially privatized companies with managers that did not know how to manage.

One must understand that in the Russia of 1995 there was a basic clash of two styles of management, of two management cultures. The old Soviet regime had managed the country by dividing all its activities into more than one hundred different industrial fields, calling them branch ministries and packing each of them with experts—each trained, naturally, only in his own narrow specialty. Many such experts were also distributed in every enterprise within a field. At this time the Government was still placing these technicians in all the companies it was still involved in, in spite of the fact that they didn't have the least bit of knowledge about the new management realities of the lean, competitive 1990s. This led to endless inevitable conflicts and inefficiencies within many concerns.

A parallel clash of cultures, another battlefield in the culture war if you will, was going on concurrently all the time within the Government, as those working day and night to privatize the economy had not only to withstand the relentless attacks of all those committed to opposing privatization, but had also to see the potential results of privatization threatened by the terrible management traditional among all these holdovers.

Furthermore, there was a different kind of conflict brewing between federal and local Governments over control of the partially privatized companies. Due to the sorts of Government mismanagement referred to above, regional governors started demanding control of the federal shares of partially privatized companies. To resolve this conflict, in cases where the federal Government didn't care about the companies in question, it did agree to hand control of its shares over to local authorities. It is interesting to note that by 1997, the federal Government had also gradually eliminated most of the branch ministries, and retained shares in local companies were mostly shifted to the Ministry of Economics. This particular ministry happened to be staffed with competent managers not bound by the old ways, and they actually began doing a good job—as, may I say, they still are.

It is almost unnecessary to note that questions related to defending national security during privatization were constantly raised by the managers who had come up through the old Soviet-era ministries. Of course they all regarded Polevanov as a wonderful ally. For many of them, opposition to privatization could be ascribed simply to the fact that when they lost the old branch ministries they felt they were losing control over these branches of the national economy, and they began to doubt their ability to protect the country from possible damage to national interest caused by the accumulation of controlling blocks of shares in enterprises of overriding importance to the nation.

It was going to be necessary to create new, innovative methods of State participation in company management. To do that, two very different impulses had to be understood, even though they often seemed indistinguishable: the desire on the part of the State not to lose control of the economy, and a basic, unreasoning negative attitude to any restructuring as such.

For example, as of 1995 we still had no civil legislation offering the most basic regulation of legal relationships in the area of land. This not only hindered the development of all kinds of market relationships in general, but resulted in considerably lower prices for the stock of privatized enterprises.

And there were other misguided political interests that never tired, for example, of putting the pressure on for granting advantages to the workers' collectives. This constantly tended seriously to distort the structure of capital stock that represented the original valuation of a privatized enterprise (generally regarded as the value of the original stock times the number of shares). As we embarked upon privatization, it was not lost on us that we were going to have to placate the workers, and we did this by allocating to them a disproportionate amount of shares. We had to do this even though we recognized that this would cause a conflict of interest in the management of an enterprise and would contribute to ineffective management. Our hope was that the workers would dilute their control of shares by selling them privately to outsiders, and that consequently the situation would stabilize and internal management conflicts would moderate.

For several years we paid a heavy price for this decision, as we waited for the workers' control to become diluted. In practice, as we all could see, the shares distributed to workers' collectives by closed subscription—where much or all of a company was offered to those inside a company at a special price before anyone outside was given a chance to buy—were usually redistributed as soon as a few weeks had passed. While it is true that the selling of these shares by workers always began immediately, the structure of a company's management could only be changed once a year, at the annual meeting of shareholders; thus it always took years to implement meaningful changes in a company's management. The workers' shares were bought either by management or by outside investors. If the interests of the management and of the outside investors coincided, a normal investment process would start at the enterprise. If not, long-term conflicts would ensue, accompanied by the usual demagoguery concerning national security.

By this period, directors' staffs and senior management of the larger joint-stock companies had become quite a serious political and lobbying force. My own view was that it was not reasonable for us to ignore their interests when developing a company's privatization plan, and our plans would always reflect the influence of these people. They definitely constituted a separate interest group; their self-interest impelled them to give priority to their retention of their control over an enterprise— *even at the expense of not attracting new investors, weakening the stock price, and creating nothing but stagnation in the company.*

This last negative tendency wasn't helping us create an efficient economy and business environment, and we had to find a way to somehow circumvent the problem; it was clear to all of us that the directorate had become a serious political and social group, and we were going to have to redouble our efforts to correct our missteps in dealing with them. Such missteps could

83

vitiate our ability to make effective decisions, so we had to prepare ourselves to think in terms of a long series of reasonable compromises with the companies' top managers.

THE BRIGHT FUTURE During the second half of 1994, we elaborated some goals of our privatization policy for the near future. For the year 1995, we proposed:

- Reducing the numbers of prohibited companies—those enterprises still treated as "untouchable" with regard to privatization.
- Increasing revenues on all levels by selling State-owned blocks of shares of newly privatized enterprises and real estate.
- Privatizing real estate, including land belonging to enterprises being privatized (prior to this time, the land associated with a privatized company was leased to the new company, but they could not sell it).
- Organizing the sale of large blocks of company stock (not less than 25% of authorized capital stock) in order to attract big investors.
- Developing and supporting the system of investment auctions, and improving the protection of outside investors by preferential tax treatment and allowing them to own land (I should add we eventually abandoned the idea of investment contests altogether, but at the time they were still useful).
- Attracting foreign investors by developing the required infrastructure—primarily banking, financial, and insurance institutions—and by creating a functioning equity market.

- Providing postprivatization support, including managing land and other types of real estate so as to help the privatized company attract additional investment by means of mortgaging.
- Improving the management of State property, including the creation of new entities capable of meaningful control over enterprises before they get privatized. The resulting improved financial performance would help to stabilize the economy by making these companies profitable before the privatization process began, and thus promoting market-oriented transformations and interim means of restructuring.
- Solving problems related to the privatization of agricultural land: Agriculture had always been divided into two parts, "Soviet" enterprises (*souhoz*) and collective enterprises (*kolhoz*). The land in the Soviet enterprises belonged to the State, while the land of the collective enterprises belonged to the collective. Of course, in practice everything was controlled by the State; but our privatization approach to agricultural holdings was to transform these structures into privatized joint stock, and to give the members first shot at all stock offered for sale. If a member wanted to sell his shares, other members had the first purchase option. Only after other members declined to purchase could an outsider procure shares. This form of privatization was a restricted partnership (*Tovarishchestvo*), a solution that left the workers a 100% right to the ownership of stock in their agricultural resource. (Unfortunately, the farmers' general tendency to refuse to open up shares to outside investment and fresh capital led to further stagnation in the agricultural sector.)

- Supporting the social sector—housing, schools, nurseries, health clinics, etc.—in the course of privatizing enterprises. These had always been created and maintained as integral parts of major State companies. It was at this time that we took what was really a deeply historic step and decided to relieve all these companies of the burden of these functions and moved this unproductive sector to local government. In cases where the local governments didn't have the resources to take over these responsibilities, the individual entities could be offered for privatization—where they would be another source of capital for the local government.
- Developing a securities market with an emphasis on development, and strengthening of the corresponding infrastructure.
- Improving the process of dealing with insolvent enterprises and creating procedures for handling bankruptcy.

CHAPTER III

THE SECOND STAGE OF MONETARY PRIVATIZATION: 1995

In January, Vladimir Polevanov was replaced as head of the State Property Committee (GKI) by my old boss Sergey Belyaev, who until then had been First Deputy Chairman, as well as Chairman of the Federal Insolvency Department (FUDN). During the discussions on Polevanov's replacement, my candidacy was considered as an alternative, but I withdrew in Belyaev's favor, as I believed him to be better qualified.

Belyaev and I keenly realized how different from the voucher stage the monetary stage of privatization would be. The former had created artificial demand—constant and fixed—while during the latter the real forces of supply and demand would be coming into play, forces we now had to learn to manage. Paramount in the new situation was the fact that an ever-growing amount of money—which, after all, can go anywhere—was flowing into the market. At the very least, we needed an accurate determination of the amount of money coming into our new system.

During the earliest stage of privatization, we had known the precise value of investment that privatization would involve: we knew exactly how many vouchers we'd sent out, the value we'd declared for them, and the single thing—stock—they could buy. Now only real money could pay for stock, and we had no idea how the population would respond. I suggested that we start by commissioning a market study to determine the current level of investment demand by individuals and corporations.

This survey would, among other things, tell us which industries were in greater demand, which would help us to gauge the amount of stock we could realistically expect to sell in a particular industry. We would also be able to project how much money the State was likely to receive from these sales. This information would become part of the 1995 federal budget.

Basing our conclusions on an exhaustive market survey, we projected that the 1995 budget would receive 8.7 trillion rubles from privatization.

The survey findings, published in May of 1995, assumed that the target figure would be met only if substantial blocks of shares in key companies were sold. This was a very painful political decision, especially in view of the weakness of the market and the possibility of undervaluing these large blocks of stock.

Small holdings are primarily for portfolio investors; they draw little interest from strategic investors, and the demand for them is always low. Large holdings, however, attract both portfolio investors and strategic (long-term) investors. The demand grows, and prices rise. Large holdings stimulated market demand and were key to implementing our aggressive program.

At that time, a 9-trillion-ruble budgetary target (approximately 1.6–1.7 billion U.S. dollars) from the sale of Government-owned stock was not at all what such a figure would mean today, because of how far we have come from the extreme political risks, inflation, and economic uncertainty we faced only three years ago.

Now, for example, it is easy to point to the tidy profitability of the sale of Svyazinvest in the summer of 1997, which alone netted a higher profit than all the State's pledge auctions of 1995 (when the banks provided the State with the capital represented by selected State stocks they would hold as security). But at that time confidence in the Russian market was really not high; consider, by way of contrast, the current value of one particular private company. In the autumn of 1997, the capitalization (the basic measure of valuation, equal to the price of one share times the number of shares) of LUKoil, the country's largest oil company, was rated on the secondary market at $1.8 per barrel of known oil reserves. Now, Russian oil reserves are renowned internationally as being second to none in magnitude, but the fact is that in 1995, all that LUKoil could bring on the market was 20 cents per barrel. (By 1997, confidence in the Russian market was so strong that even at $1.8 we didn't sell.) That in a nutshell is why 8.7 trillion was, at that time, an almost unthinkable amount, and why the fact that we were able to generate 8.7 trillion rubles in 1995's sales of Government-owned stock is almost incredible. I consider the 1995 results my greatest achievement.

As I said, selling major blocks of shares was a painful political decision. And just at the moment when we had to come forward with this idea, which we knew would be met by fortissimo outcries, I suddenly had to take over (temporarily) as GKI Chairman. My boss, Sergey Belyaev, was appointed First Vice Chairman of Russia Our Home, the organization of the political movement we were part of, and I had to take over, feeling as if I had been left virtually alone to carry out our plans. It turned out to be a little reminiscent of what had happened to me back in St. Petersburg, as I not only had the main responsibility but gradually again became the prime point man and public target in the area of privatization politics. I would miss Belyaev's talents as a manager and executive; but the Parliamentary elections were approaching. The Kremlin had set up two moderate groups, on the assumption that the extremes of left and right were nothing to be overly concerned about. The center-right organization, under the leadership of Viktor Chernomyrdin, was Russia Our Life; the center-left one, under Ivan Rybkin, was known simply as the "Ivan Rybkin movement." (The Kremlin's confidence in the stability of the political center as embodied by these two groups was shattered by those crazy elections, which were won by Vladimir Zhirinovsky and the Communists.)

PRIVATIZATION AFTER THE EXPIRATION OF THE VOUCHERS: OBJECTIVES FOR 1995

Once again, I would like to review the main objective of the second stage of privatization: achieving a rational balance between fulfilling the financial objectives of the budget and gaining investment support for companies undergoing privatization. This objective was the foundation of privatization in the second half of 1994 and throughout 1995. It was reflected in the major economic decree signed by President Boris Yeltsin on July 22, 1994, which contained the following provisions concerning the privatization of state and municipal enterprises after July 1, 1993:

- Rejection of numbers-based privatization—i.e., the drastic, vast simultaneous "forced-march," "collapse-type" form of privatization—in favor of a planned and consistent process of restructuring and attracting investment.
- Reduction in the advantages granted to employee groups, with a matching increase in the number of shares allocated to investors.
- The sale of shares in large blocks, i.e., 15–20% of a company.
- Allocation, within the company itself of the bulk of the receipts (51%) obtained from the sale of shares or property assets of a company undergoing privatization .
- Expanded rights for privatization authorities at the regional and local levels.
- Valuation estimations for all companies undergoing privatization, using a standard method of assessment based on a reappraisal of principal fixed capital assets and on stock-price history after being offered for sale.
- Intensive privatization of real estate, including land.

It was proposed that the bulk of privatization revenue in 1995—6.85 trillion rubles—would be derived from the sale of shares of oil companies that had been established and were being restructured, part of the overall goal of 8.7 trillion rubles. To do this it would be necessary to sell State-owned property assets worth 24 trillion rubles—an amount almost equivalent to the entire IMF credit. As mentioned above, 51% of the receipts were earmarked for the companies, and only 10% (2.5 trillion rubles) could, according to current law, be assigned to the federal budget. We had to change the law, so that urgently needed funds could be quickly distributed among the local budgets, the budgets of the federation members, as well as among the State Property Committee (GKI), the Committee for the Management of State Property (KUGI), the Russian Fund for Federal Property (RFFI), and other bodies.

And we knew that there was only one way of achieving such a rapid and sharp increase in revenues: the massive sale of blocks of shares in the oil companies assigned to federal property. The remaining revenues would be obtained from the sale of shares in other enterprises undergoing privatization including those under the temporary control of RFFI, the sale of land owned by these enterprises and of their incomplete construction assets, from rental payments, and from the redemption of leased property.

The breakdown of potential investors was as follows: foreign firms, 34%; investment departments of banks and private individuals, 25%; former CHIFs undergoing conversion into investment companies, 10%. (A bit of information, to avoid needless confusion: "CHIFs" were the voucher investment funds mentioned earlier; "voucher" was the informal, if universal, way of referring to our great invention, giving rise to the acronym VIF, for voucher investment fund. "CHIF" was an alternative expression for the same thing, based on "privatization check," the official designation just about never used in conversation.)

Bear in mind that the shares of enterprises undergoing privatization had a lot of competition on the market. This competition included State securities, both federal and local, and shares of private issuers including second and subsequent issues, shares of banks, bearer bonds of speculative structures of the "MMM" type, and shares of financial and investment companies and pension funds.

However, our main competition was undoubtedly foreign currency—above all, the U.S. dollar. This concerned mainly private individuals, who even today prefer to invest their savings in dollars. The amount involved was some 30–40 trillion rubles. In the event that inflation was halted, it was a safe bet that this money would go into the equity market, including into shares of enterprises undergoing privatization. Unfortunately such thinking remained purely speculative—and one could wait indefinitely for its realization.

Although Russia's financial market was just emerging, all its instruments—foreign currency, stocks, credit, *veksel* (promissory notes), securities markets—became important channels for financial transactions. Given the rapid growth in the number of players in Russia's financial market, which by the way was steadily developing in almost every region of our vast country, we expected a substantial increase in the number of Russian companies receiving licenses to trade in securities. We therefore also expected a sharp increase in the sale of shares of enterprises undergoing privatization, which could lead to an upset in the balance between supply and demand.

This was why shares had to be sold gradually, keeping careful pace with the development of the infrastructure of the securities market. Over a long period of time, this approach would make steady income for the budget possible, that is sales of relatively small blocks of state-owned shares—though at prices much higher than in the current market. And new shareholders would constantly be joining the ranks of those personally involved in the structure and management of privatized enterprises. This careful pace would also allow us to gain time as we fine-tuned the new infrastructure of Russia's securities market and prepared Russian investors for active involvement in cash auctions.

In order to maximize the financial results of the sales of State-owned blocks of shares, it was necessary to develop a marketing strategy in which the need to inject planned amounts of revenues into the federal budget would go hand-in-hand with related but not identical goals such as achieving the highest possible price. To these ends it was going to be vital to organize the distribution of shares on Western securities markets.

According to international practices, a massive sale of shares is usually preceded by efforts to raise the price of shares previously issued, in order to maximize the profit. It is not customary to sell shares when the price is falling. In 1995, the price of almost all shares of privatized enterprises in Russia was quite low. Attempts to sell a substantial part of blocks of shares of privatized enterprises, when neither the market nor investors were ready for this, would have resulted in the fall of prices of shares of privatized enterprises during cash auctions. Prices might even fall far below current low levels, in which case the State wouldn't receive the income that would have been derived from the gradual sale of shares.

Unfortunately, purchases of blocks of shares in Russia's key enterprises at rock-bottom prices at cash auctions was a reality we had to deal with, and with it the strong possibility that key blocks of shares might land in the hands of investors not interested in the growth of Russian joint-stock companies. This uncertainty was partly due to the fact that we hadn't totally recovered from the shock of 1993, when Government security forces had to attack the Parliament building, with worldwide live TV coverage. In addition, the various shocks of 1995 were already starting: the Duma elections and the period of sky-high inflation (which reached at its highest point an annual rate of 2,000%) and high Government short-term bond (GKO) rates. In such an atmosphere stocks in general were of no serious interest and the prices were low. This tendency held true throughout 1996, by the way.

So we realized that broad simultaneous cash auctions of State blocks of shares in enterprises undergoing privatization were out of the question. We needed to do long-term work, clearly targeted and detailed. In order to conduct the cash auctions more efficiently, we deemed it necessary to fulfill certain conditions:

First, we had to continue developing the infrastructure of the Russian securities market: the legal underpinnings for the regulation of securities operations still needed much work; efficient stock exchanges and systems for over-the-counter trading had yet to be created; and depositories (bodies for guaranteeing payments and for recording the transfer of share ownership) had to be carefully developed.

Second, it was necessary to increase the volume of transactions involving shares of privatized enterprises (according to the experts, such transactions in 1994 totaled approximately half a billion to two billion dollars). Previously, only small blocks of shares in privatized enterprises had been sold at cash auctions. Russian investors were still not ready to invest in the shares of privatized enterprises, since they felt there was no certainty that they would be able to sell the shares later on the financial market if they wished. Hence, Russian capital was directed into GKOs; this was more profitable than putting the money into industrial companies. Realistically speaking, we knew that as matters stood only foreign investors aiming at portfolio (speculative) investments or at the control of key segments of Russian industry were ready to invest in the share capital of privatized enterprises.

Part of the shortfall consequent to our decision to postpone cash auctions could be offset by transferring State-owned shares in privatized enterprises into trusteeship or by receiving credits from banks based on the government's pledging of these shares to the banks.

Accordingly, developing an investment policy in 1995 required a lot of creative work. The State Property Committee needed to work actively with branch ministries and committees. In our investment programs we were aiming at specific market possibilities, rather than groundless appeals by issuers for resources. That is, in order for our auction strategy to work, plans had to be specific and appropriate, in terms of which enterprises to privatize when, and what size investment was needed for each enterprise. During the voucher period, committees had been set up for specific industries; now there were special committees that would take individual enterprises and bring them through the whole privatization process. It was costly and laborious; but these were major companies, and so satisfying results were expected.

In trying to better coordinate planning our auctions with the actual needs of the companies, we were at the same time always encouraging the new kind of management our businesses have to have today in order to deal with current realities. We needed to find out from management what investments were needed, but if we had just waited for their wish lists, we would have ended up just financing more of the same old inefficiencies—typical requests had to do with fixing leaking roofs or replacing machines. We were learning to turn the question around and be more aggressive, asking *them* what new products they could see themselves producing and what new materials, equipment, and structures they would need to start.

By implementing a realistic investment program, companies could hope to assure themselves of steady and stable sales of products in a long-term market, rather than just capital renewal;

an investment program, in any case, is not essentially intended to solve the day-to-day financing of the enterprise.

In a drastically inflationary period like the one we were living through, the financial aspects of even the most ordinary day-to-day processes are thoroughly distorted. By the time raw materials become finished products, the return isn't even enough to buy new raw materials, let alone make a profit; "investment" goes straight into these new raw materials and not into new fixed capital, endangering the future of the enterprise.

The data we received on more than 500 key national enterprises, and enterprises with the most attractive investment prospects, indicated that their total investment need was some 40 trillion rubles. These enterprises were about to spend 25% of investments received on new construction (10 trillion rubles), 51% on acquiring new products and therefore on modernizing their production facilities (21 trillion rubles), 5% on developing the social sector (1.8 trillion rubles), and 18% on reconstituting working capital (7 trillion rubles).

For a long time, the market culture of our management was below any civilized standards. In 1995 only one fourth of all enterprises had development programs that could realistically be called "business plans." Only half had any notion of development strategy. The rest did not have the faintest idea of their future prospects. Against this background, managers proposed investing 0.4% of capital to improve management structures. For a long time, management simply blocked privatization, favoring instead the disintegration of the economy that would be the result of forming closed-type companies. One reason was that the State never seemed to bring careless or unskillful directors up on administrative or criminal charges. I personally think that the State and such a director should really have contact in only a few areas: timely and full payment of taxes, execution of contractual obligations, respect for labor and environmental laws, security arrangements, etc. The rest is the business of the owners of the enterprise—shareholders, trade unions, partners, and all those whose legal rights are either respected or violated by the director. These people have many ways of exercising their influence—and will employ them, because their direct interests are at stake—ranging from damaging the firm's reputation to dismissal at a shareholders' meeting.

All these circumstances obviously called for coordinating work in the areas of procedures and practices among the State Property Committee, the Ministry of Finance, the Federal Commission on Securities and Equity Markets, and the Central Bank.

We had to make sure our sales policies were well-formulated and easy to understand. Additional investments depended on making the financial numbers available to the investor, as part of our effort to inculcate an atmosphere of rational planning and well-timed sales. This was encouraged as well by our "open policy": not only were we constantly absorbing new data from the economy, but we were absolutely determined that no one should find the activities of our Committee anything but totally open, above-board, transparent, and public. We knew that we had not only to meet the demand for our shares, but also in many respects to generate that demand as well.

Besides developing a detailed schedule, we decided to introduce a special system of informing investors. This included an optimized structure of information for different investors geared to their different profiles and different ways of seeking out and receiving information, whether in national magazines, local newspapers, or the Internet; optimized channels for gathering information on investments; and a computer network which coordinated all this data and accessed it for the actual investor. (In the end this computer system never got built: we were counting on a German credit that was ultimately not granted. And it was our fault—we didn't pay enough attention to it.)

Considerable work was needed to draw up a series of regulations and standards for the securities industry. These would include regulations governing the early sale of blocks of shares in enterprises previously fixed in federal property and the amendment of standards fixing the allocation of funds. We could no longer defer the drafting and enactment of a law on trusts, the sale of land as part of the overall property assets of the enterprise, or the deregulation of selling fixed assets. It was necessary to extend legislation on privatization to sectors that were not traditional for us: State insurance companies, State blocks of shares in banks, and so on.

Finally, in the event of a fall in the inflation rate and a rerouting of private individual capital back to the equity market, it would become necessary, in order to attract this individual capital to shares of enterprises undergoing privatization, to develop a large network of all-Russian specialized cash auctions, similar to the voucher auctions.

SALES STRATEGY IN 1995

Our story gained in dramatic intensity when we heard that the political foes of privatization in the Duma had played what they thought was a very neat trick on us. Yes, we and they had concurred on the projection for revenues from privatization and fixed it at that 8.7 trillion figure in the Budget Law for 1995—but they had turned around and simultaneously banned the sale of oil company shares during this period, exactly what they knew we needed. Our objectives immediately became almost impossible to meet.

I am convinced that the two decisions were related. Nobody ever talked about it openly, of course, but I could tell—it was a game. Until 1995, the Communists and others had been saying that privatization wasn't working, that it didn't benefit the budget. As the budget for 1995 was being debated in the Duma, they were threatening to put a stop to privatization altogether. Our Committee asked them: What will satisfy you? And they said: How much can you raise? Give us a commitment for the '95 budget. So we looked at all the big chunks of stock we thought we could sell, including oil company stock, and came up with the 8.7 figure, itemized by company, and submitted it to the Duma. No one objected, no one *could* object, as this was an admirable sum. Now, the aim of many in the Parliament has always been to discredit privatization, so they became very worried that we would fulfill the goal—because that could really legitimize privatization. They couldn't very well object to the number, so they hit on the clever idea of writing into the law this little ban on sales of oil company shares, exactly what we had projected would supply us with 70% of the revenue! Our numbers had been accepted, but we had been deprived of the means of achieving them.

During the coldest winter months, January and February of 1995, we struggled with the problem. We knew that if we failed they would have us for dinner. Then, in March, at a Government-sponsored bankers' meeting, one of the representatives of the banking community, Vladimir Potanin, the President of the UNEXIM Bank, suddenly had a bright idea. He suggested, "If you can't sell those shares, why not give them to us as collateral and we will extend you loans that will enable you to meet your target." And so was born the "loans for shares" program, also known as the pledge auctions of 1995—the topic of Chapter IV.

On May 11, 1995, President Yeltsin issued a decree entitled, "On Measures to Ensure the Flow of Receipts from Privatization into the Federal Budget." This gave privatization fresh momentum, as it revoked all previous decisions on fixing blocks of shares in federal property, i.e., excluding strategic industries from privatization, increased the normative portion of privatization revenue that went into the federal budget, and allowed for lower prices to be paid by privatized enterprises to gain title to their land.

The Russian Marketing Association conducted a broad survey of the Russian securities markets, covering a wide spectrum of potential investors, which helped us to determine the investment demand structure: how much capital investors were ready to invest, when, and into what instruments. The findings of the survey provided the basis for the strategy of cash privatization during the second half of 1995 (which was structured in time, by economic sectors, and by blocks of shares). In August, sales of blocks of company shares were scheduled for September through December of 1995. The list included 136 large Russian enterprises. Among them were EES Rossii (Unified Energy Systems of Russia), the LUKoil and YUKOS oil companies, the Svyazinvest stock company, maritime and river shipping companies, the nuclear power industry, precious-metal mining companies, airlines and airports, chemical and manufacturing plants, and fuel and power plants.

The Russian Fund for Federal Property (RFFI) was instructed to put maximum effort to make sure that generous blocks of shares heretofore legally fixed in State ownership got sold, as well as various shares still held by RFFI and appropriate property

101

funds. Stock sale dates were set for the period between August and October that included sea, river, and air transportation firms, the timber industry, fuel and power plants, chemical complexes, the natural gas industry, and telecommunications companies. The RFFI, really an administrative arm of our Committee, was also charged with monitoring sales schedules in the various regions and issuing reports every two weeks.

In 1995, the Russian market was on the rise, and didn't experience the crises racking the world market; it turned out to be able to accept the quantities of new stock we were going to offer, even while the world market fell. The cumulative demand of foreign and Russian investors, banks, and the population was evaluated at no less than 19 trillion rubles. This was more than enough to sell the amounts of property we had designated for sale, get full value for our oil shares, and receive our 8.7 trillion rubles.

It was just about at this point that I said at one of our quarterly general news conferences, open to all the media, that I would accept "the axe" if we didn't meet our goals. All I meant was that I would accept being fired, but for some reason the newspapers reported that I had "agreed to be executed on December 15." I guess some people will always think that's what I said. In any case, at a moment as historic as this, when our goal was nothing less than to make the rolling back of the Communist Revolution irreversible, a little cooked-up melodrama was perhaps appropriate.

CHAPTER IV

THE PLEDGE PLAN

"The loans-for-shares plan came from our enemies."

These days, there are always a few people whom the media in their infinite wisdom decide to quote in great quantity—or misquote—for a while. I gather that in the West when people talk about getting their "fifteen minutes" they are referring to this phenomenon.

Frankly, I hope my turn is over.

But like it or not, as point man for privatization it was my lot to be in this position in Russia for a certain period. The reader witnessed this when I supposedly "agreed" to be "executed."

Now, the quote that heads this chapter was one I liked quite a bit more (let's say it's one I cooperated in propagating, so I guess I must have). It's about Vladimir Potanin's bright idea that saved us, to the consternation of those enemies—who naturally never stopped criticizing us, no matter what we did.

The trick they had played on us and the brilliant one we found to return the favor may provoke a chuckle or two now—but before this and other battles were won this was a very serious game indeed, make no mistake about it, and played for unimaginably high stakes.

"LOANS FOR SHARES" is what the ads we took out in newspapers all over the world called it. These were certainly three of my first words in English.

We called them pledge auctions, which was what they were.

The fateful meeting during which the idea emerged of the Government receiving credits—large loans—in exchange for blocks of oil company stock not sold but pledged, i.e., held by the party extending the credit as security for the loans, took place when representatives of a group known as the Consortium of Russian Commercial Banks came to meet with the Government. At the time that group consisted of the following banks: Imperial Bank, Inkombank, UNEXIM Bank, Stolichny Bank for Savings, MENATEP Bank, and the joint-stock commercial bank International Company for Finance and Investments.

Out of that meeting came Decree No. 889, "On the Procedure for Pledging Stock Held in Federal Ownership for the Year 1995," signed by President Boris Yeltsin on August 31, 1995. This step not only served to guarantee our ability to fill State coffers and meet our obligation to the budget, on which so much depended. It also represented a breakthrough for the equity market, creating at a stroke the conditions necessary for the real emergence of players interested in taking part in the new, "normal" economic system. The end result was nothing less than major growth in the capitalization of Russian joint-stock companies, exactly the factor that we felt would make privatization irreversible and Communism a dead issue.

The decree had already gone through different versions, and the final one had certain very specific advantages. One was the public and truly competitive nature of the process of granting pledge rights; another was the technical feature that it was not the entire property of an enterprise that was pledged but only the State-owned block of shares.

The Government's obligations were limited. Bear in mind that at the expiration of the term of the loan in a future year, not only the term of the loan but also the ban on the sale of oil shares that our friends in the Duma had hung around our necks would have expired. Taken for granted was the idea that if by that time the Government had "failed in its obligation" (let's just say this was something we more-than-half-expected—after all, the point was to inject huge sums into the budget, not pay them out), the holders of the shares would assume actual ownership of the shares, and could sell them.

Thus in this pledge structure the participating banks had three functions: guardian, temporary owner of the shares, and, in case of failure to pay, the brokers ("commissioners") in selling those shares.

It was agreed that at that point, if the amount of money obtained from selling the block of shares was insufficient to cover the credit—i.e., turned out to be less than the amount that had been advanced to the Government during the year 1995, the Government bore no responsibility to the creditor.

This condition was a beautiful thing: what it meant was that, as a result, during the term of the credit these banks would be doing their best to make sure that at the end of the term, those stocks were worth a lot, by participating actively in the long-term planning on the part of the company—just the kind of active, creative shouldering of responsibility for making things grow and work that we wanted so desperately to inculcate in our fellow citizens, especially those in positions of economic power.

The State Property Committee carried out tenders for two kinds of rights. The first was the right to get the block of shares in question as a security, together with certain rights in their management, with some exceptions. (For example, without prior written permission from the Committee, a pledge could not vote at a shareholders' meeting on certain questions, e.g., for the restructuring or dissolution of the company, modification of statutory documents or bylaws, etc.) The second right was that of a commissioner, i.e. the right to act, after a certain time, on the instructions of the Property Fund, as a seller of that block of shares.

As it developed, most of the banks ended up with pledges representing majority control, and they proceeded to send in their own managers, which we viewed as a very positive development.

Participation in the tender was open not only to the members of the Banking Consortium, but to all other players on the equity market as well. Whoever could offer the largest amount of credit at a fixed rate and fixed term won the tender. These were the only criteria for selecting the winner.

We felt that the scheme was in keeping with international standards of equity-market operation and could be considered as an advance payment to the investment intermediary, who could at a later time play the role of the seller of the block of shares in question, acting in the name of the State. The commission agreement assumed that the agent, who either was the creditor himself or had a contract with the creditor, could sell the pledged shares, with the result that the Russian Federation's debt would be retired. The agent had the right to decide how he would sell the stock, choosing among the methods stipulated by the Russian privatization law (with the exception of investment auctions).

It was also stipulated that 30% of the positive difference between the stock selling price and the amount of debt of the Russian Federation would be the agent's profit, while the remaining 70% would go to the federation budget. (Talk about a good deal.)

The list of companies to be sold under the pledge plan was based on the proposal of the Consortium of Banks and determined by individuals of their choice. I must point out that it was not Kokh or Belyaev or Chubais who decided which enterprises were to be privatized, and this is a very important point. Privatization was to be based on Federal laws and Government acts, not on the whims of the State Property Committee. Privatization plans usually appeared after someone said they would like to buy a particular enterprise and was prepared to pay a particular amount of money for it. At this point we would consider whether the offer was a fair price for the entity or the property was worth more. What would this prospective buyer do with it? What was the potential downside of the deal? Only after due consideration of such questions could a coherent privatization plan be generated and approved. Based on the procedures in place, privatization plans were not going to be the fruit of Kokh's or anybody else's inflamed imagination. They were always built upon specific proposals.

As one would imagine, the companies proposed by the Consortium of Banks were the crème de la crème of the Russian economy. The financiers wanted to control stock that would yield solid profits and would be worth something in the event of a default. (The banks received dividends during the pledge, as compensation for the fact that the interest rates involved were quite low.) The proposed list consisted initially of 43 stock companies, all likely to be very attractive to investors. Companies in the defense sector would still be under State controls in certain ways having to do with the filling of defense orders and safeguards against takeover by foreign individuals or entities.

The final version of the list, which appears in the Instruction of the State Property Committee of September 25, 1995, consisted of 29 enterprises. Later, by a special Presidential decree, eight of these were taken off the list, allegedly for national-security reasons. This was one of those moments when all kinds of "patriots" come out of the woodwork—I was always amazed at their number. These were the people running the companies at the time, claiming that they were "the best managers in the world" and not in need of private entrepreneurs. Since by that time—the special decree was issued in December—we had already skimmed most of the cream off the pledge auctions and privatized them, the omission of eight enterprises from the list was not a major event, and we refrained from getting into disputes with the managers and politicians involved.

A special interdepartmental commission was established to conduct the pledge auctions. I was the chairman; other members were representatives of the Ministry of Finance and other agencies that had been running sales of property, such as RFFI, the Property Fund.

From the point of view of protecting State interests during the implementation of the pledge plan, setting the starting prices was important. One had to take into account the likelihood of collusion among the bidders (later events confirmed these fears). This is why it was important to establish a starting price that, on the one hand, would not allow the participants to get the stock as security at a very low price, and on the other, would attract a large circle of investors to participate in the auction. In setting the starting prices, we took into account international and Russian experience with collateral crediting against shares, according to which if the object of pledge consists of readily available assets, the credit amount varies between 60% and 90% of their market price, depending on the size of the block.

Later analysis showed that starting prices had been based on market quotations at the time. The enemies of pledge auctions verified this some twenty times over, and finally had to give up. It was a humiliating defeat for them. Their claims that we had understated the prices were completely unfounded (although some of them still claim I "sold State property down the river"). At that time the degree of capitalization of the market was very low. It is worth noting that the starting prices proposed to the Commission by the Bank Consortium were two to five times lower than the ones eventually confirmed by the Commission.

The amount of credit corresponding to each block of shares could not be lower than the starting price. The interest was calculated on the ECU equivalent of the credit, at the rate of LIBOR (the London Interbank Borrowing Rate) plus 0.5% a year, for three-month deposits. As a result, the State obtained credit at an interest rate that was two or three times lower than the market rate. The money had to be transferred within ten days after the credit agreement was signed. The earliest date for the selling of stock was first fixed at January 1, 1996. Later this date was postponed to September 1, 1996. Personally, I was already convinced that pledges would not sell the stock right away. The future proved me right.

GENERAL DESCRIPTION

By January 1, 1996, we had held 12 pledge auctions, selling the stock of such companies as Surgutneftegaz, a huge integrated oil company; Norilsky Nickel, a mining company; Severo-Zapadnoye Parokhodstvo, a shipping line; Mechel, iron and steel; LUKoil, an oil company; SIDANKO, a Far Eastern and Siberian oil company; Novolipetsky, a metallurgy complex; Murmanskoye Morskoye Parokhodstvo, another shipping line; Nafta-Moskva, an oil products trader; Sibneft, an integrated oil company; and YUKOS, also an integrated oil company.

Bids had been invited, but no applications came, for four other lots: Kirovlesprom, Tuapsinsky Morskoy Torgovy Port, Bor, and Arkhangelsky Morskoy Torgovy Port. Apart from the fact that investors were not overwhelmingly interested in those enterprises, I should also mention that we set the prices so high that few were willing or had an opportunity to participate in the auctions. I suggest that the small number of bids shows that we were selling enterprises at sufficiently high prices. One must admit, on the other hand, that having restricted the foreigners' access to certain lots, we were indeed left with only a limited internal market for these companies.

For seven out of sixteen auctions, participation was allowed only for Russian bidders (LUKoil, SIDANKO, Norilsky Nickel, Novorossiyskoye Morskoye Parokhodstvo, Murmanskoye Morskoye Parokhodstvo, YUKOS, and Sibneft). This was fiercely attacked by the foreign media, who did not hide their irritation, even though this was the first such ban in the three years since the beginning of the privatization campaign. As I have already said, up until now Russia had conducted a most open policy regarding foreign investments. Even most of our defense enterprises, if not all, were sold with no restrictions on foreign investors' participation. (This has indeed led to a number of problems with our military and security services, whose criticism was sometimes well founded.)

Now, for the first time, we set a precedent by banning foreign participation in a privatization operation. Let me emphasize again, though, that the exclusion list consisted of the world's major oil companies, with enormous oil resources and therefore enormous potential.

I knew well enough the privatization history of the countries in Eastern Europe, where restrictions on foreigners' participation existed from the very beginning and were quite strict. Yet despite these restrictions, foreigners invested much more money in those countries than in Russia while I was running the privatization campaign. I believed that a ban on foreign participation in the privatization of strategically important companies of this kind was justifiable for more than one reason: even though foreign investments are an important development factor for countries with a transitional economy, such a huge country as Russia will not survive on foreign investment alone. We had to work on creating a *Russian* capital base, and a certain dose of healthy protectionism was undeniably necessary.

I don't mean to say that foreign capital shouldn't participate in the privatization of Russian oil companies; only that it should be done on a somewhat different basis than in the case of other industries—in particular, after production-sharing arrangements have been made in the accepted international manner (American oil companies' production-sharing agreements with Middle Eastern oil companies being perhaps the best known). Nor did I rule out the possibility of creating consortiums to finance various oil projects in which foreign participation could play a strong part.

111

But during those early days of oil-company privatization, under-capitalized Russian financial institutions and entrepreneurs could not compete with foreign capital, and in order to ever be able to compete in the future, our oil companies had to be kept in the hands of Russian investors.

On several occasions in the course of the "pledge auctions saga," some people proposed that auctions be put off for various reasons, particularly due to the current status of the Government short-term bond (GKO) market. My position on this issue was firm and definite. Strictly speaking, it was not my task to protect the Government short-term bond market. My responsibility was to sell off Russia's assets at the highest prices possible to raise stock quotes for Russia's privatized industrial companies. In a certain sense, these two markets are competing with each other. If, at a certain moment, the Government bond market is doing well (prices are up and therefore interest rates are down), then generally, the stock market for privatized enterprises tends to stagnate—and vice versa. Evidently, by November 1995, our day had come. Shares became more attractive than Government bonds. What could I do about it? Note that stocks became more attractive even though they yielded lower returns than the Government short-term bonds. Something else must have attracted our investors.

Under the circumstances, I thought that the Central Bank and the Ministry of Finance should have a system in place to look out for the well-being of these competing markets. When the Finance Ministry issued Government short-term bonds to the market, it unfortunately did not coordinate its decisions with our sales schedule. We weren't able to say, "Listen, we're selling Rostelekom now—could you please wait with the Government short-term bonds to give the institutions and individuals with capital in the Russian economy a chance to use it for the purchase of our new shares?" Nobody has ever been willing even to consider the wisdom of this option. The coordination of our activities has never been considered by senior Government officials, so we simply had none—and we have often hurt each other's offerings.

Actually, I myself was asked several times to postpone pledge auctions (in particular, the YUKOS auction). But I didn't consider the arguments offered convincing, and didn't want to postpone anything without clear instructions from my direct superiors, which never came. If I had, in fact, agreed to help keep up the prices of short-term Government bonds, it would have meant I had conceded my goal of adding the maximum amount possible to privatization revenues. That was my job, and I didn't feel it was for me to suddenly change its nature. I did agree to put off YUKOS for two or three weeks, but on one condition: I asked that my target of nearly nine trillion rubles be reduced by at least a trillion. This would have taken some of the pressure off my department and enabled us to seek higher prices for the smaller supply of stock we would be adding to the marketplace.

OUR ERRORS

Unfortunately, we could not totally avoid making errors while implementing the idea of pledge auctions. We lacked experience in carrying out operations of this kind. Also, UNEXIM Bank was inefficient in its role of representing the State Property erty Committee. We encountered a number of serious problems, like authenticating the documents submitted by applicants, problems related to compliance with bank guarantees and other legal norms, or such aspects as determining the exact time for transferring the advance to the appropriate account. A number of provisions in different documents relating to the rules for conducting the auctions contradicted each other. Worst of all, we also felt that insufficient information had been supplied to us about the companies whose stock was being pledged. And the advertising campaign connected to these auctions was probably not as convincing and aggressive as it could have been.

Finally, we cannot ignore the negative effect on public opinion that the position taken by the so-called Consortium-2 (made up of Rossiysky Kredit, Inkombank, and Alfa Bank) had. Lacking the money necessary to participate in bidding for such expensive and attractive lots as Norilsky Nickel, YUKOS, SIDANKO, and Sibneft, these banks engaged in scandal-mongering and pseudo-"investigations." Though they were not the only ones, these people made a fine art of floating rumors of all kinds and promoting them in the press—even making sure they came up in the Duma. And then something like the following would happen. Here they were, with the Rossiysky Kredit bank having just offered $355 million for Norilsky Nickel. Then they were supposed to deposit $350 million for YUKOS: all three of these banks together were unable to come up with the money.

Some issuers were not disposed to stock auctions because of the way we put revenue for the budget first as a priority compared to investments. These issuers proposed to place conditions on participation, demanding that the participants invest in the enterprise itself, including the social protection area. In several such cases, the investment amounts in question had to be equal or greater than the market price of the block of shares being pledged. The Russian joint-stock company Norilsky Nickel went as far as proposing to include in the conditions the "immutability of the Board of Directors."

NORILSKY NICKEL

Immediately after it had become known that the state-owned block of shares of the Norilsky Nickel joint-stock company would be put up at a pledge auction, I received a letter from its president, Anatoly Filatov. He expressed his doubts concerning my position and that of the State Property Committee in this matter.

It would be ridiculous to suggest that I disliked Norilsky Nickel, or that I was insensitive to the company's recurring problems. Filatov knew it better than anyone else. (For the purposes of the auction it meant nothing, for example, that this Anatoly Filatov was indeed that very executive in the Arctic region who'd insisted on building a furniture factory in the frozen wastes, thousands of miles from the nearest tree; he even had the old Soviet look about him—one of these physically massive men with an exaggerated sense of their own infallibility and untouchability that matched their girth.)

No, I made it a point of being impartial, simply promoting what we had to sell. Together, we laid down the legal basis of the company's operation, agreeing on our positions at arbitration, in Governmental hallways, even before the President himself. I even put in a lot of effort trying to convince Anatoly Korabelshchikov, the President's personal aide for relations with the provinces, that our way was right. Korabelshchikov had been with Yeltsin all the way back his early days in Sverdlovsk, before it reverted to Yekaterinburg, and though he possessed neither talent nor personality he had remained by the President's side, where he never tired of trying to influence events by whispering rumors and negative opinions in Yeltsin's ear.

My position regarding the incorporation of Norilsky Nickel led to a serious conflict with Valery Zubov, the Krasnoyarsk regional governor, who had for ten years been a personal friend of mine, all through my academic years, a professor of economics at Krasnoyarsk University and a very intelligent man. He has my respect as an effective governor and more, but he is a facilitator rather than a leader, perhaps a bit of a fence-straddler, and found it necessary to go to both Yeltsin and Chernomyrdin to complain about me; for a while he found it impossible to shake my hand in public in spite of our old relationship. I was seriously troubled by all this—but it did not affect my position on Krasnoyarsk Non-Ferrous Metallurgical Works.

Krasnoyarsk Non-Ferrous is a platinum-refining division of Norilsky Nickel, which extracts 40% of the world's platinum production—that sounds great but demand is narrow and production costs very high. (A note: this particular market may change now, as batteries worldwide are being made with longer-lasting platinum, and world platinum prices have risen 30%.) Norilsky itself is a holding company with the main factory at Norilsk in the Arctic region, refining works in southern Siberia near the Chinese border, two nickel factories in the Kola Peninsula near Norway, and an engineering institute in St. Petersburg.

I was proud to sit on the Norilsky Nickel board of directors, proud to be a real working member rather than a VIP invited for the show, proud that I could play a constructive role in its work—as long as the Government held a large stake in the concern and I was the Government's designated representative. Many people—perhaps including Filatov—had trouble believing that an out-of-towner like myself could take to heart Norilsky Nickel's problems. But nobody could claim I was insensitive to these problems. On the other hand, how could I help wondering about the business-like, peaceful atmosphere that extended through all board meetings (attended by the directors of all the factories and representatives of other industries), lasted through the only order of business—Filatov reading aloud his report followed always by the unanimous vote of approval—and continued with blissful consistency through the cognac and hors d'oeuvres that always ended the meeting in such a pleasant fashion?

There were a number of questions on which I felt I could have reached an understanding with Filatov and his deputies. In my opinion, further neglecting the company's problems would inevitably result in an economic disaster on a grand scale. I was deeply convinced that without a hands-on professional effort the company had no future, and it may be my fault that I could not convince Filatov how grave these problems were.

First, there were problems of cash-flow management. Norilsky had no financial policy then, nor a financial management program in general for any part of the foreseeable future. What was called "financial policy" was a policy of patching holes, of emergency all-out borrowing without exact calculation of the funds' repayment. This was true in regard to both credit institutions and business partners, relationships that had long been based on what can only be termed "caveman's barter." It applied as well to the social sector, to "North delivery" problems (i.e., the well-known difficulties of doing business in a place where the main transport arteries—by sea and river—are frozen and unavailable much of the year), and to the attitude toward the budget. In my view, the gravest was the latter.

To clarify the lack of a financial policy: for one thing, there was no coordination or integration. Each affiliated enterprise had its own independent financial policy, at least for borrowing, and never notified the president of the company about problems until after they had already occurred. The sheer number of persons making decisions in the area of borrowing resulted in the policy being completely irresponsible. Such mechanisms as temporary transfers of free funds between affiliates did not function at all. Instead, affiliate enterprises took credits, and this was on its way to resulting in bankruptcy, due to high interest.

I often raised the question of the solvency ratio of Norilsky Nickel's affiliates at the board meetings, but this information was not furnished to all members of the board of directors, neither the year when I raised the issue nor a year later. It certainly looked as though I was the only person interested in this information.

My preliminary analysis had shown that the current liquidity ratio or coefficient of solvency (the ratio of working capital to financial obligations) of all affiliate enterprises of Norilsky Nickel, except perhaps Krastsvetmet and Gipronikel, was below one (the standard value is two). This means that the Federal Insolvency and Bankruptcy Office could raise the question of bringing an action for bankruptcy at arbitration. I didn't think this was part of their plans.

I was starting to fear a replay of the sad story of the YUKOS company, whose management discovered that its main affiliate enterprise, Yuganskneftegaz, was bankrupt. (In Russian law, there are several levels of bankruptcy. In "absolute" bankruptcy, creditors sue and the court creates a committee of creditors to run the enterprise for 18 months to try to get it out of its mess and then reviews the situation again; or the court directs a sale of the enterprise at auction to cover debts. Another level consists of various forms in which bankruptcy can be declared by the enterprise itself. In this particular case a holding company—YUKOS—took action against one of its enterprises—Yuganskneftegaz—and as the majority shareholder dismissed management and appointed its own management team. All these stories are from the preprivatization period.) The YUKOS management hadn't known that Yuganskneftegaz had a $30 million customs-tax arrears plus a $90 million penalty on that sum. This was equal to half of all YUKOS's yearly exports!

To give a contrasting example, I would cite LUKoil as an example of unified cash flow. Even though it had budgetary problems, they were nowhere near the scale of YUKOS's, and were dealt with openly and in sufficient time for help.

Another problem was the market value of shares. No other company in the Russian over-the-counter market had such disgraceful rate fluctuation as Norilsky Nickel. This happened while the world nickel prices were growing steadily, at least during the second half of 1994 and first half of 1995. I want to emphasize again that what happened to Norilsky Nickel's shares was a national shame, suggesting a complete irresponsibility and lack of professionalism on the part of its management. To fall from 80 thousand rubles a share down to 23 thousand rubles—taking inflation into account—is equivalent to an eightfold drop in price in one a year! Even taking into account political risks, this was unprecedented and unnecessary.

I said many times that in order to raise share prices they needed to develop a program. But mine was a voice in the wilderness. There was no program whatsoever; the share-price behavior was monstrous and could lead to accumulation of stock belonging to workers of member companies in the hands of ad hoc or irresponsible groups, even criminal structures. We know well that many of these hovered around nickel exports.

Every day, confidence in Norilsky Nickel's stock fell even lower. What kind of appeal could Norilsky have for private investors? How was Norilsky Nickel going to attract investments by selling securities? Was the State budget going to remain the major investor of one of the potentially most profitable of Russian companies? This really endangered the future of privatization.

The recipe for stabilizing the price of shares can be found in any textbook on securities. Personally, I explained the technique many times. First, one has to choose an internationally acknowledged registrar with authorized capital of at least 200 million dollars. There was such a registrar of security contracts in Russia, created by the Bank of New York, and I tried to get Norilsky to transfer their register of shareholders to this registrar, but it still remained in Unikombank. I had nothing against Unikombank, but in this particular case its renown as a registrar was not sufficient to help stabilize the share price. Unfortunately, the management of Norilsky Nickel did not want to understand such things. To them it all sounded like nonsense, while the technical problems of register transfer frightened them very much. In short, they didn't think the problem of stabilizing the share price was sufficiently important for them to have to actually move their rear ends.

The second aspect of share-price stabilization is ensuring the open nature of the business. It is necessary to give as much information as possible about the enterprise to the media; and the more economic data that become public, the better it is for the share price. No investor will ever buy a pig in a poke! This is the A of the ABC's of the stock market. And also why I considered the nomination of Coopers and Lybrand as Norilsky's official auditor in May 1995 an important success for our side. One could not overestimate the importance of this decision.

Norilsky Nickel was potentially a very profitable enterprise, but it found itself in dire straits. Therefore, it seemed logical to put it on the list of enterprises that could profit from collateral crediting against their shares. The auction to sell 38% of the Norilsky Nickel stock took place on November 17, 1995. In fact, there were only two real contenders: the UNEXIM and Rossiysky

Kredit banks, but it was hard to tell because of all the smokescreens. Applications were filed by UNEXIM, whose guarantor was the International Finance Company (MFK), by MFK with UNEXIM as a guarantor, by Reola with MFK as a guarantor, and by Kont, whose guarantor was Rossiysky Kredit. These 38% of shares of a major nonferrous metallurgy complex, the total amount of whose yearly production is comparable with the budgets of some of the CIS countries, had a starting price of $170 million, which was extremely low.

As I examined the bids closely, I smelled a rat. According to current laws on banking, the total amount of guarantees issued by a bank could not be greater than the guarantor bank's capital itself. However, it was found that the $170-million guarantee issued by Rossiysky Kredit to Kont was $70 million greater than the bank's own capital at that moment. Other guarantors' capital seemed credible. The commission decided that there was an explicit violation of the auction rules on the part of Rossiysky Kredit. The president of Rossiysky Kredit, Vitaly Malkin, demanded that this problem be solved by swapping the roles of the contender and the guarantor. He was claiming that Kont had about 200 million dollars of its own capital. However, this procedure was not stipulated by the auction conditions, and they were not allowed to participate in the auction.

The auction was won by UNEXIM Bank with a bid of $170.1 million (with a the starting price of $170 million). Immediately, Vitaly Malkin put on a big act. He publicly tore open his envelope and read the amount they had planned to offer: $355 million. This allowed him to claim that we had poorly defended the State's interests. The State was said to have lost $185 million as a result. However, I fear that had we made concessions to Rossiysky Kredit, we would have run the risk of not getting anything at all from this auction. How was I supposed to believe in their $355-million myth when I hadn't seen a guarantee for the $170 million? If there was ever a case of a bird in hand being worth two in the bush...

I must admit that in the end, the Rossiysky Kredit representatives showed some common sense and did not file a lawsuit. The lawsuit was brought by Norilsky Nickel itself. This was the first in a bunch of "pledge suits." The company brought multiple suits: against the State Property Committee, to overrule its Rules of Conducting Pledge Auctions Protocol No. 2 on the results of the auction and the pledge order to the registrar; against the Ministry of Finance, to nullify the credit agreement with UNEXIM Bank; against RFFI, to nullify the commission agreement; against UNEXIM Bank, to nullify the pledge agreement, credit agreement, and agreement of cession of right to make a commission agreement; and against the "MFK/Moscow Partners" Bank, to nullify the commission agreement. The plaintiff argued that the pledge auction was a cover for a sale of shares, which means that the deal should be declared null and void and the sides reset to their previous states. The plaintiff tried to prove the illegality of orders and agreements which were, in fact, in full compliance with standard forms stipulated in the Presidential decree on pledge auctions. Notice that at the same time the plaintiff did not dispute the legality of the decree itself nor was the intent to bring suit against the President of Russia!

In February 1996, Moscow City Arbitration dismissed the case. The representatives of Norilsky Nickel were not satisfied and lodged an appeal. However, two other courts took our side. It could not have been otherwise. The plaintiff tried to prove the illegality of orders and agreements which were in full compliance with standard forms stipulated in the Presidential decree on pledge auctions (again—remarkably—the plaintiff did not dispute the legality of the decree itself). They had the nerve to do all this, in spite of the fact that somewhat earlier the board of directors had deemed pledge auctions legal enough to write some by now well-known letters to the Government asking that the auction be conducted in certain ways that they preferred!

YUKOS

In my mind, the pledge auction of 45% of the stock of the YUKOS oil company is linked to being sick with flu. Indeed, I was running a 105-degree fever at the time of the auction, and could barely stay on my feet. Aside from that, the auction, which took place on December 8, 1995, did not go smoothly. The 45% block of YUKOS shares was acquired by an unknown company at the price of $159 million (the starting price was $150 million). This phantom firm was LAGUNA, which served as an agent of MENATEP Bank. At an investment auction taking place simultaneously, LAGUNA offered to invest $150.125 million (the starting value was $150 million), and acquired a 33% block of YUKOS shares. Babayevskoye, representing the interests of Inkombank, was disqualified.

Initially, the terms of the auction had required that the bidders' funds be deposited in the MENATEP bank; but Alfa, Rossiysky, and Babayevskoye had raised hell about having to deposit money with one of the bidders. And they were catered to—a decision was taken that the money had to be deposited at the Central Bank, our Federal Reserve. This was revealed as a very negative development for them when they learned that only cash can deposited at the CB.

All participants in the investment contest had been required to deposit $350 million in the Ministry of Finance account at the Central Bank. MENATEP had simply complied with the condition, while Inkombank, together with Rossiysky Kredit and Alfa Bank, did not, for lack of funds. Instead, they appealed to the State Property Committee, asking to be permitted to deposit Government short-term bonds instead of cash, and presented a statement of deposit of $82 million at the Central Bank together with a statement to the effect that they were holding $370.2 million in Government short-term bonds.

It was no mystery to us that if such permission were granted, MENATEP would file a suit against the State Property Committee. So we asked the Ministry of Justice to give us their opinion on the subject. Minister Valentin Kovalyov responded in person. Depositing Government short-term bonds instead of money would be too significant a modification of Central Bank rules, and therefore could not be permitted. Hence, Babayevskoye was disqualified.

In principle, all of these banks could have participated in the acquisition of YUKOS. They could have gone to the Central Bank and obtained a certificate to the effect that a certain amount of Government short-term bonds, the full equivalent of $350 million, was actually on deposit. Then they could open a serious discussion, retain competent lawyers, and establish rules for depositing the bonds in a special account at the Central Bank. Should someone else have done all this for them? God helps those who help themselves. Instead, we were shown a certificate to the effect that they had a certain sum in Government short-term bonds on account at the Moscow International Currency Market. It had been on their demand that MENATEP had deposited the money in an independent account at the Central

Bank, but they were content to let Babayevskoye use its own facility.

Thereafter, Inkombank, Alfa Bank, and Rossiysky Kredit could not collect as much money as YUKOS and MENATEP could obtain, for instance, against oil futures. All sorts of things become possible when such an oil company joins forces with a large bank. This made people angry, and they started repeating angry mantras like "if we could only separate YUKOS from MENATEP" and the like. But strategic alliances are legal, and play a positive role.

Notice that of two possible options of conducting that auction—with or without the participation of Babayevskoye—we chose one that reaffirmed the auction's legal standing and protected it from a potential lawsuit.

Our decision turned out to be right. Babayevskoye lodged a complaint at the Arbitration Board against the State Property Committee and RFFI, in which they put forward the same objections as were later exposed in a letter of the Procurator General, Yury Skuratov, to Viktor Chernomyrdin. During the session of March 28, 1996, Moscow City Arbitration considered this complaint and dismissed it, thereby accepting the actions of the State Property Committee and RFFI as justifiable.

The arbitration found an absence of illegality in the actions of the State Property Committee. This was of extreme importance to us. We were dead sure that the decision would have been different had we admitted Babayevskoye to the auction: MENATEP would have filed suit. But we were able to establish our impartiality and our singleness of purpose: our only motivation was a wish to secure the necessary revenues for the State budget in the most correct and legal fashion.

SIBNEFT The controlling block of shares of Sibneft, perhaps the most scandal-prone Russian oil company, was offered at a pledge auction on December 28, 1995. The starting price was $100 million, which was essentially based on the market value of the stock of two major structural divisions of Sibneft: the Noyabrneftegaz Production Association ($130 million for 51% of shares), and Omsk Refinery ($55 million for an equal block of shares). Noyabrneftegaz is an oil extraction company, Omsk a refining company. They are both in Siberia.

These were the main bidders before the auction: Stolichny Savings Bank and Oil Finance Company, Ltd., Inkombank, SAMEKO (whose controlling block of shares belonged to Inkombank), Tonus, and MENATEP. In fact, MENATEP participated in the auction only to back the Stolichny Savings Bank group and the Oil Finance Company—a tactical maneuver in case there would be only one participant (in which case, according to the rules, the auction would be called off).

Fifteen minutes before the auction started, SAMEKO bowed out. Inkombank was barred, since its package had failed to meet the registration deadline (the bank guarantee and balance did not satisfy the requirements, and the amount of its proper funds did not allow Mosbiznesbank to issue a $100-million guarantee to Inkombank).

As a result, the Sibneft shares were acquired by the group of applicants consisting of Stolichny Savings Bank and Oil Finance Company, who offered a credit of $100.3 million dollars. Right after the auction results were made public, the Inkombank representative tore open his envelope and read out the sum of $175 million. This happened from time to time at the auctions, when the fellow who has been disqualified dramatically tears open his own bid envelope and reads this great bid the Government has just passed up by being pigheaded and unfair. Of course, since the fellow is among the losers, he will never actually be put on the spot and made to prove that he can actually cough up the money, that he actually has it. Such grandstanding is very safe.

Inkombank considered its rights had been violated and saw no other course than a lawsuit. We were ready, having had litigation with Norilsky Nickel and YUKOS. Once again, Inkombank filed a complaint at Moscow City Arbitration, lodging the same claims as it had in the case of the YUKOS auction. However, in this case the first-level court decided that the State Property Committee decision of not admitting Inkombank to participation in the contest was illegal. This ruling was without precedent. For the first time, the results of a pledge auction were canceled. Moreover, a dangerous precedent was set. Losing one auction could endanger the others. However, the State Property Committee won the cause on appeal at the Appellate Board of Moscow Arbitration, which agreed with our argumentation and on July 22, 1996, overruled the first decision

Thus, we—the State Property Committee—won all arbitration proceedings on the results of pledge auctions. These efforts did not hold up in court, and we were able to say that we had never broken a single law. The Arbitration Court simply confirmed this fact.

Certainly, it was natural that the way the auctions were organized would lead to different reactions from a number of banking and entrepreneurial structures. Certainly, we committed some real errors in organizing auctions; but another reason for this reaction stems from forms of business competition considered normal only in Russia. Then—as now—entrepreneurs were more willing to appeal to the Government and to the law-and-order agencies than to courts.

When conducting pledge auctions, the State Property Committee renounced this kind of shifty procedure and based its actions on a different idea, the idea of legality. This was something we felt people had to learn more about anyway, if the economy was to move toward what we considered normal functioning. We were in the spotlight and on the spot, and felt it behooved us to set a couple of precedents on our own; putting the idea of legality in a central position was one of them. Every time a conflict emerged, we aimed our effort at winning through arbitration. Time eventually proved us right.

In speaking of the general results of pledge auctions, we should not forget that the end of 1995 was by far not the best time for privatization in Russia. In December '95 the Duma elections were won by the Communists, and there was the additional shadow cast by the impending Presidential elections that would be taking place in June–July 1996. Suffice it to say that the above-mentioned restrictions on the participation of foreign investors were a decision that we were partially forced to take. On the one hand, we had to prove that our office functioned well (even though I think we had proven it many times already); on the other hand, I did not think that it was reasonable to have to prove the feasibility of privatization at the cost of wild political scandals. But this was exactly how the whole situation looked from the outside. Even Vladimir Shumeiko, who had signed hundreds of privatization orders, including ones concerning strategically important enterprises, when he was the First Deputy Prime Minister in the Government, suddenly started sharply criticizing that same privatization which had been carried out by himself and others. I will not even mention the inveterate enemies of the State Property Committee who were constantly criticizing us in the State Duma.

Someone said that all that (i.e., pledge auctions, some lots being canceled and some others emerging, dates being changed) smacked of children's games. But I knew that this was no playground; these were men's games, played hard and fast. At one meeting the Prime Minister told me that I would answer with my life for all that goes on around privatization. If these were children's games, where were the adults' games? The situation was not simple or funny. Things were sad. And grave. Much more so than people could imagine. But I have always been an optimist, and so I was not going—as some well-wishers were advising me—to eat my hat or commit suicide.

The memories left by the pledge auctions are still vivid. Even though today we can hear practically only one opinion—that they were pure nonsense—I disagree. Certainly, in many aspects they were an artificial procedure. This was due to three distinct factors: mutually contradictory laws, a vital need for budget income, and a deadly opposition. Yet we managed to solve the problems we faced, legal as well as budgetary. By pledging State-owned blocks of shares, we obtained credits whose total amounted to more than one billion dollars, 70.8% of all privatization income for 1995. Of this sum, 3,574 billion rubles was received as direct credits and 1,526 billion rubles was received in the form of the cancellation of companies' indebtedness to budgets at federal, regional, and local levels.

After the pledge auctions, violent discussions started as to whether we could consider the money received as privatization profits. I thought such discussions pointless. A budget is like a pool with two pipes: water goes in by one pipe and goes out by another. It does not matter what name one gives to the "water" that goes into the budget—taxes, privatization revenue, excise duties, or fines, as long as the basin is getting filled, allowing water to go out. Hence, I did not care how this money was entered in the books—privatization profit or taxes—as long as it came in. Who is to take credit for paying off trillion-ruble company debts in a matter of days? Is it Internal Revenue, the State Property Committee, or the Ministry of Finance? Certainly, a part of the credit belongs to the Internal Revenue Inspection, but the property it worked with was State property, more precisely State-owned securities. This is why I was not trying to convince anybody that the money came from privatization. In my mind, I knew it was so.

Our campaign aimed at borrowing financial resources was extremely effective. At that time this was a realistic—and the only noninflationary—source of financing the budget. Limiting the participation of foreign capital was justified. As the auctions showed, Russia already had its own private investors who were capable of investing up to $200 million in the stock of privatized companies. In addition, this money was deflected from the market of Government short-term bonds. It was important that we managed to show that we could bring hundreds of millions of dollars into play in our national economy.

Some things do not have a stable valuation, and this is true worldwide. How many people can attach an objective value to a human life? The idea is absurd. For us in Russia, there were likewise other things that we had no way of valuing or understanding. One was the idea of property; and until we had some idea of that we were certainly going to have difficulty understanding what a stock is. We did know these things existed. We knew there was $200 million sitting in the banks. Now these millions would be put into play, making industry and the economy hum with new

130

vitality, while still giving the Government the use of the money to pay teachers and nurses as well.

According to my good and close friend Anatoly Chubais, the choice wasn't between selling at ideally organized auctions, with absolutely fair price competition, and selling in conditions of compromised integrity. The actual choice was different. We could sell for money or not sell. The second option meant letting the property be stolen, that's all. At that time (a moral note of considerable historic irony), selling for money was already a step in the direction of greater integrity.

Finally, the President himself spoke on the results of pledge auctions. He declared that he supported privatization, which, he said, was one of the major directions of the economic reform being carried out. He called the plan of pledge auctions "generally correct," and recommended that we use the experience thus gained when deciding on the forms and methods of conducting privatization in 1996. Some changes were to be made in the rules of applying for participation in auctions. As for the forms of payment for the stock, people had to be allowed to pay in Government short-term bonds as well as hard currency. The President expressed his conviction that "pledge auctions have a future in our country, and after certain improvements in the rules, they will continue."

CONVERTIBLE BONDS In March 1995, the Government of the Russian Federation issued a decree entitled "On Measures of State Support for the LUKoil Petroleum Open-Type Joint-Stock Company and Its Affiliated Enterprises." The decree contained a decision to call for investments necessary to conduct a technical reconstruction of LUKoil-affiliated enterprises. LUKoil wanted the State to back up its bonds, in case the company got into trouble; so they issued the exact same number of bonds as the State held shares in LUKoil. In the case of a default, the shares would be used to pay creditors. The company bonds would be negotiable both in Russia and abroad, and the shares would be temporarily fixed as State property, amounting to 11% of the capital stock of the companies.

These bonds were supposed to be exchanged for the companies' stock deposited in a financial institution after the end of the term during which the stock had been held by the Government. The bonds were distributed on a competitive basis among underwriters, who had to place them on the secondary market.

Everybody was happy with the results of the first stage of the contest, which took place before the end of 1995. Out of 350,000 securities with a nominal value of 4.5 million rubles, 320,000 were bought. The buyers were well-known investment banks and financial companies. As a result, the federal budget received one trillion rubles. The second, Russian branch took place later. Its volume was 110,000 securities, and one bond was exchanged for 170 shares.

This was the first time that convertible bonds were issued in Russia. Before LUKoil, nobody in business in Russia had ever used this tool.

(Note: To tell the truth, I personally opposed this idea; indeed, what happened was that eventually the State did end up having to cover the bonds with its shares.)

**SVYAZINVEST
1995**

In 1995, we thought we could sell 49% of the shares of the Svyazinvest stock company at a commercial investments auction.

Our first try, when we attempted to sell a 25% block of shares, became one of the most celebrated and analyzed failures of that period.

The 25% project was one of the very first examples of privatization on a project-by-project basis, with a solid presale preparation. The Russian Privatization Center, entrusted with developing the plan, called for tenders to find a finance consultant. Among the participants figured the world's biggest telecommunication companies. Especially active in the final stages were German, French, and Italian companies. The International Financial Corporation of the World Bank and the European Bank for Reconstruction and Development even expressed their willingness to acquire Svyazinvest stock on the same conditions as the winner, which could be considered as a confirmation that the contest was conducted according to world standards.

The tender was won by a consortium of investment banks and other investment structures headed by NM Rothschild & Sons. The obligations of the winner included the presale preparation. The major problem of that was a matter of taking peculiarly Russian issue-related information and presenting it in a form suitable for the Western market. The winner also had to find a buyer and ensure the guarantees, as well as conduct the contract process. The time given for all this was a single month.

The Svyazinvest auction took place on November 30, 1995. It was won by STET, an Italian company and one of the biggest telecommunication operators anywhere (fourth in Europe, sixth in the world). Selling a 25-percent block of shares of Svyazinvest

133

was the first project on such a grand scale. Its purpose was to fill the State budget and to create a Svyazinvest investment fund. The budget component of this deal was equal to $770 million, or 2.9 trillion rubles. Of that sum, 1.5 trillion rubles were earmarked for the federal budget.

We had every reason to believe that before the end of 1995 the State Property Committee would be able to direct the funds received from the deal both to the federal budget and to the Svyazinvest investment fund. Anatoly Chubais called the project "the first real privatization result." He should have never said it—but it was too late to avoid the jinx. The deal came to a halt when, at the very last moment, the buyer made significant additional demands of the Russian side. These demands were twofold: that the money be put in escrow abroad, and that all member companies of the Svyazinvest company (i.e., about 80 companies in all) be internationally licensed. Complying with the latter condition would have taken at least a year; as for putting the money in escrow, this was unacceptable for us in principle. The deal did not go through.

Why? One reason is that the final stage of the project was held at the same time as the elections to the Duma, where the best showing was made by the Communists, headed by Gennady Zyuganov. The Liberal-Democratic party came in second, the Russia Our Home movement third; Yabloko, the party headed by the liberal economist Yavlinsky, came in fourth, and Gaidar's party did not obtain any seats at all. The opposition won a resounding victory—and we have been reaping the fruits of this disaster ever since. No matter what others may say, I remain deeply convinced that the final decision of STET not to pay for the block of shares they acquired was affected by the election results.

Although all the preparation work we had done failed to produce a contract, on the whole this was a very important positive experience. The applications of the auction participants helped establish new privatization prices. According to the STET bid, telecommunications companies were assessed three to four times higher than the existing exchange quotes. Unique experience was gained in preparing and conducting a large international investment auction whose conditions were open and equal to all participants and that was accepted by the leading world companies. All objective observers agreed that the failure to conclude the deal could not be imputed to the Government—whose behavior had been absolutely correct.

NATIONAL AND REGIONAL SPECIALIZED AUCTIONS

As time went on, the privatization process changed, first from vouchers to cash auctions, then on to specialized events whose purpose had less now to do with property reform and more to do with fulfilling budgetary targets.

And the mentality of buyers was changing. They started to look much closer at the quality of properties offered at auctions: the operational capacity of industrial installations, the market value and yields of the stocks, and the lack of restrictions on stock-related rights to participate in the company management. Specialized auctions were not a distribution of property anymore but, rather, an important component of the equity market. In this way they closely linked privatization to the general direction of the State's financial policy, which dominates the equity market via currency regulation and the system of State debt. Put simply, for the first time privatization started looking for money in the same pocket as the budget does when it is looking for sources of covering the deficit, and as private structures do when they seek resources for industrial investment and financial operations. We were slowly turning into a normal, Western-type financial system.

The preparation of properties for sale at specialized auctions, including the choice of dates and volumes, was carried out by the State Property Committee and regional property management committees.

Unfortunately, starting in early 1995, we witnessed a decrease of money inflow to the Russian equity market. There was a sharp drop in the volume of both Russian and foreign investors' orders for Russian stock. Attempts made by some big investment and brokerage companies to enliven this sector of the financial market did not bring the desired results. Most investors preferred to work with State bonds, which were more reliable and, at that moment, more profitable. The growing supply at the end of the year and the fact that most important Russian companies took their stock to the market after they were privatized did not lead to an increase in the volume of investment. The reason was the political situation in Russia.

The hopes that investment money would come from a wide range of population, i.e., that people would put their money into shares of privatized enterprises, were to a large extent overly optimistic. By the time the specialized cash auctions began, people had another, more reliable way of investing the disposable money, that is, in State savings-loan bonds. Income derived from these was more tangible and easier to obtain. More than 50 issues of municipal bonds were also registered. In May of 1995, municipal bonds were granted the status of State securities. This whetted investors' appetite for them still further.

People did not trust corporate securities, and the insufficient development of the equity market infrastructure prevented them from selling small blocks of shares on the secondary market to get at least some kind of an income. That is why at this time there was no increase in demand for the stock of privatized enterprises on the part of Russian investors. Besides, the money turnover on the private securities market went down because of inflation.

As far as foreign investments were concerned, not only did their volume fail to go up as predicted, but it went down even further. Sales of stock by foreign portfolio investors to Russian companies on the secondary market became a typical phenomenon. This tendency could be traced rather clearly. The main reason for the quotes going down and staying low was that the demand on the internal market was very low, while the foreigners were timid and inactive. They sold shares to our brokers and to small investment companies, which resold them immediately. The market was slack. A daily turnover of $1 million is not much; today it reaches $200 million a day.

The gap grew between the benefits one could expect from stocks coming on the market during privatization and those from State bonds. All governments have deficits, and bonds are issued to deal with them and bring the budget closer to balance. Later the bonds will be honored; in the meantime more are issued. We studied what other countries did, and we realized that there are many thousands of institutions that buy such bonds. We also understood that there is a certain amount of money that Russia at this point would be capable of attracting. And we were offering two different products to attract it (industrial shares and treasury bonds) that clashed, in a way. In general, the portfolio investors preferred by far to purchase treasury bonds because they are guaranteed by the state.

My own view was the following: I believed that the Russian Government had to have a unified, coordinated policy of offering those two instruments to international investors. Without such a unified policy we would always discover that a new bond was being issued the day before our block of shares went on sale. At this point in our present story *no one* was saying there should be a unified policy; and the Finance Ministry really was affecting our ability to make investing in mining in Siberia look exciting—at the very least, it didn't help our efforts to sell shares as part of privatization.

Investment opportunities for private citizens are another resource not yet used to full potential. These include a promising mechanism for drawing money, the share investment funds (PIFs). These function in the same way as mutual funds do in America. To this day, not much progress has been made on these. There are a dozen licensed PIFs that sell shares, but none of this is very serious yet. Theoretically, PIFs appeared in Russia immediately after the passing of the Securities Market Law and the President's Decree concerning the creation of the Federal Securities Committee at the end of 1994. They really hardly exist in our country even now, and they are certainly not playing the role they should be playing and were intended for, i.e., attracting individual savings. In the United States, mutual funds attract more individual savings than the whole of the Savings Banks system. In Russia, the ratio is one to a million.

But things are changing. Only a year ago, the very idea that one day the Government short-term bonds would be less profitable on the securities market than corporate shares was considered a pipe dream. We used to debate about far-off times when these two sectors would start competing with each other. Today, it is evident that the profits are higher in the corporate market than in the Government short-term bonds market.

During the entire year of 1995, only 23 blocks of shares were sold at national and regional specialized auctions of RFFI through the Federal Stock Corporation (see Table 1). The stock from state-owned blocks, offered for sale at cash auctions, can be divided into two large groups. The first includes liquid shares, i.e., shares of companies that show an active turnover on the secondary market. The second group includes nonliquid shares, i.e., shares that have limited turnover on the secondary market. There were few people who sold or bought them, which led to a decrease in the number of would-be participants in the auctions. There was a third group of shares, those offered for sale on the equity market for the first time. One could form an opinion about the liquidity of these shares only after one saw more of the reaction of market participants.

The party most interested in the shares belonging to the second group either was the issuer himself, who, as represented by the company management, wanted to protect himself from an outside investor by increasing the size of his own block of shares; or it was a direct investor, whose goal was buying a large block of shares in order to gain management of the whole company. The auctions of stocks from the first group were better at drawing money into the State budget. Apart from the issuers, stocks from this group attracted portfolio investors.

The population itself was supposed to become participants in auctions. The very idea of selling State-owned blocks of shares at specialized cash auctions allowed a small investor to put disposable money into shares of privatized companies. However, he could not do it if he had to buy shares on the secondary market, since most secondary-market operators work with large holdings.

Most companies offered for sale at specialized cash auctions through the Federal Stock Corporation belonged to the nonliquid category. The first sales of this type of stock started before the emergence of temporary methods of defining the starting price at an auction. At the first stage of sales, setting the opening prices at 20 times the nominal ones proved to be acceptable, since it was simply impossible to objectively define the market price of shares that had never been negotiated on the secondary market. On average, in the first series of auctions stocks were sold at 2.5 to 3 times the opening price.

Later, after the State Property Committee elaborated methods closer to market criteria, the opening price was defined through taking into account the sales results of first lots, the prices of stock of comparable companies, property evaluations, and ratios provided by branch departments.

The results of national and regional specialized auctions are clearly illustrated by examples of stock sales of the largest Russian privatized companies, such as Rostelekom, EES Rossii (Russian Unified Energy Systems) and KomiTEK.

The national specialized auction at which a block of shares amounting to 0.9% of the authorized capital stock of Rostelekom was offered was held in 40 regions of Russia. There were 466 applications, with 400 from individuals and 66 from legal entities. The latter, nevertheless, represented 83% of the funds. Only a few regions took an active part in the auction—St. Petersburg, Nizhny Novgorod, the Volgograd region, the Krasnodar region, and the Urals. The bulk of the funds came from Greater Moscow.

The Rostelekom specialized auction is interesting because its stock was quoted on the market. The block of shares offered had a strong effect on the secondary market, its size representing about one third of the number of shares negotiated monthly on the secondary market. The resulting price of shares at the end of the auction was only 10% below the price on the secondary market at that date.

The all-Russian specialized auction in which 4.5% of stock of the EES Rossii joint-stock company was offered took place in more than 50 regions of Russia. This stock was quoted on the secondary market, too. But just before the beginning of the auction, the capital stock of EES Rossii was multiplied by 308. The initial selling price was set at 500 rubles per share, which corresponded to the nominal cost. In theory, taking into account the situation on the secondary market, the initial price should have been set at one-fourth or one-fifth of the nominal cost. Only 13.8% of the block of shares put on sale was sold. Had the capital stock not been increased, the same sum of money could have been obtained only if four times as many shares had been sold.

The national specialized auction in which 4% of stock of KomiTEK was offered also took place in more than 50 regions of Russia. The timing of this auction was poorly chosen. At the end of the year most investors lack funds. Besides, blocks of shares of big oil companies such as SIDANKO, Vostochnaya Oil Company, and some others had already been offered at specialized auctions in November and December of 1995. This made the block of KomiTEK shares look less attractive, especially against the background of the ongoing specialized auction of Sibneft stock. There hadn't been enough time for presale preparation, either.

The initial price at this specialized auction was set at 980 rubles, i.e., one-third of what it would have been at the cash auction that had never taken place. Even so, only 1.34% of the 4% of authorized capital stock was sold.

Some of the shortcomings of the normative basis also made the shares sold at specialized auctions less attractive. Among the most important shortcomings were (a) the possibility of a split based on the results of a specialized auction rather than on the decision of a stockholders' meeting, as is required by the law on stock companies; (b) the absence of regulations concerning the register holder's obligation to make necessary changes in the register and to provide specialized auction winners with excerpts from the register at a time stipulated by the law; (c) the absence of normative documents concerning authorized depositories at RFFI and the State Property Committee. The problem of computing auction rates did not always have a solution, given the existing normative basis.

The market efficiency of national and regional specialized auctions was ensured primarily by a wide network of stock supply to the market and by easy access to auctions. Because the auctions went far beyond the limits of the already existing secondary market, which was cornered by big capital operators, it became possible to hold and to bypass the market rates when selling stock of the above-mentioned companies. At the same time, the results of the KomiTEK auction clearly demonstrated how the price and the number of shares sold depend on the timing of sales and the presence of competing bids.

The peak of sales at national specialized auctions coincided with the pledge auctions. In both cases, the biggest financial effect came from oil companies. The weighted average selling price of oil companies' shares negotiated at specialized cash auctions was only 10% below their price at pledge auctions, though the stocks offered at pledge auctions were more attractive, as they belonged to the biggest oil companies with high market liquidity.

FINANCIAL RESULTS OF 1995

In 1995, privatization income came to be considered one of the major sources for covering the deficit in both the federal and local budgets. One cannot analyze the extent to which we patched up the budget without considering the normative basis that regulated sales of State-owned stock and other property. Some of these normative acts were, in turn, approved because of insufficient rates of meeting the budget.

The implementation of the decree "On the Procedure for Pledging Stock Held by Federal Authorities for the Year 1995" in November and December 1995 resulted in federal receipts of over 5 trillion rubles, i.e., 70.8% of total privatization income. I am convinced that only a lack of time, along with active opposition of a number of branch ministries and local administrations defending their corporate interests, prevented us from getting significantly larger revenues.

As far as the volume of sales was concerned, nationwide and regional specialized auctions became the leading method of privatization. They provided the second source of budget revenues, immediately after pledge auctions. In 1995 we organized 4,114 cash auctions, 833 specialized auctions, 555 investment contests, 84 commercial contests, 1,634 sales by closed subscriptions, and 1,714 sales through the Enterprise Employees Corporation Funds (FARP).

Investment auctions and commercial auctions with investment conditions resulted in the winners offering more than 2.5 trillion rubles and almost 2.5 million dollars in investment. Eighty percent of privatization income came in during the last two months of the year, which indicates the importance of careful planning and monitoring of this process.

The absence of bids at some of the auctions can be easily explained. Either the offered blocks of shares belonged to "dull" stock companies, the initial price of stock was too high, or one sole investor possessed the controlling block of shares. For example, the controlling block of shares of the Era stock company in the Leningrad region already belonged to the German company Henkel; consequently the auction, which was to take place on November 3, 1995, and where the initial price and the nominal cost of one share were set at 1,000 rubles, did not take place at all. (Among "dull" properties were the casualties of history—rather modern factories in the very highly advanced military-industrial complex for whose products the demand had fallen, for obvious reasons. The Russian economy is one-third the size of the American, but its military-industrial complex is *equal* in size to that of the United States. So these great modern factories have limited value: they go begging.)

During 1995, the projected income from privatization was corrected after we took into account important cuts in the list of types of property that could be sold (for example, the ban on selling shares of oil companies), decrees of the Russian Government approved in September 1995 that concerned structuring oil companies, and the above-mentioned slowdown of investment demand.

Finally, the 1995 federal Budget Law fixed the revenues from sale and use of State-owned property at 4,992 billion rubles, where 82.6 billion rubles came from dividends on shares reserved in federal property. One hundred twenty-three and eight-tenths billion rubles had to come from rental payments and redemption of pledged property, and 4,785 billion rubles was the income from sales of State and municipal property. Altogether, the State Property Committee delivered 7,467.4 billion rubles, or 150% of the projected amount, to the federal budget. Apart from the income coming from pledge auctions, this sum included the proceeds from the sale of bonds of the LUKoil company (one trillion rubles) and of property at all hierarchical levels (1.14 trillion rubles) (see Table 2).

The experience of meeting the budget target for the year 1995 showed that in the future, the implementation of large projects of the Svyazinvest and LUKoil type, together with pledge auctions (especially if we learned from our failures), could become major sources of privatization revenues.

QUANTITATIVE RESULTS OF 1995 By January 1, 1996, there were 118,797 privatized companies in Russia, or 56.7% of the total number of enterprises that had been State property at the beginning of the privatization process. The privatization dynamics of enterprises is shown in Table 3.

The analysis of privatization dynamics of enterprises shows that the privatization rate in 1995 dropped compared to the previous period. This was due to the fact that most companies in the register of corporate enterprises had already become stock companies.

If we analyze the distribution of privatized companies by type of property by the end of 1995 (Table 4), we can see that in 1995 most privatized companies (83.3%) emerged from former municipal property.

On January 1, 1996, the general register of enterprises included 34,762 corporate enterprises. Of these, 27,774 (79.9%) were already registered as joint-stock companies; 1,591 enterprises were included in the register in 1995.

By then, controlling blocks of shares of 3,659 enterprises had been allotted as State property, including 321 enterprises just in 1995. And the golden share was retained in 1,190 enterprises, including 67 in 1995.

As earlier, the major type, of advantages were granted to employee groups during incorporation according to Plan Two, i.e., one where employees enjoying the same rights could buy up to 51% of company stock. This privatization option was chosen by 72.5% of workers' collectives. Plan Three was much less popular, chosen by only 2% of companies.

ADVANTAGES OF PRIVATE PROPERTY

By 1995, it became clear that generally the privatized companies performed much more efficiently than those remaining in State ownership. Privatization had become the basis necessary for making enterprises more vital. Studies conducted by the Leontieff International Center for Social and Economic Research on 266 companies from eight industries in thirteen regions showed that:

- The integral economic index of privatized companies with more than 25% State participation was 1.43 times higher than that of State-owned enterprises, and for privatized enterprises with less than 25% State participation it was 1.57 times higher.
- Economic efficiency of privatized enterprises with more than 25% State participation was 21% higher than that of State-owned enterprises, and for privatized enterprises with less than 25% State participation, it was 42% higher.

- According to financial stability indices, privatized enterprises with more than 25% State participation did 5.41 times better than State-owned enterprises, and privatized enterprises with less than 25% State participation did 2.18 times better.

What can we conclude? One thing is indisputable. Having acquired a real owner, privatized companies start working better than State-owned ones. There is nothing more damaging for an industry than anarchy, irresponsibility, and lack of a clear perspective. Companies that passed through the "time of troubles" in a fast and thoughtful manner soon started to reap the fruits in the form of investment, secondary issues, stable outlets, and new technologies. This did not come out of the blue; these things came together with a new ownership structure, with the appearance of foreign investors and managers who felt an incentive for creative work. At the same time, companies whose management screamed hysterically about "national security," where fighting for control was more important than shareholders' rights, plunged into dead-end crises, production dismantling, and increasingly deeper indebtedness.

I am profoundly convinced that no functionary of any level will ever be able to manage an enterprise better than a private owner. This is logical, for such is the nature of private interest. Privatization is the only realistic way toward production efficiency. When we have an efficient market, we will have taxes, social programs, good defense capacity, science, culture, and many other good things.

BANKRUPTCY OR NOT

Certainly, there were cases when a privatized company didn't work well. Its problems may have been caused by any number of possible factors. I firmly believe that in no case was it ever related to the factory having become the property of a private person, and have never felt that such an enterprise should be returned to State ownership.

Why? Imagine that someone has bought a small factory from the State. Maybe he did not pay too much money for it, but it was his own money. He wants to make the factory profitable, in order first to break even, and then to make a profit. This is how an average entrepreneur reasons. However, after a while he understands that he made a mistake. For various reasons, however hard the guy might try, his factory cannot make a profit. And I daresay that this entrepreneur tries hard, because it was his own money he spent. At that moment comes a State functionary who tells the entrepreneur that since he did not succeed, the State will take the factory back from him, and then our small factory will immediately become a gold mine! This is where my comprehension stops. Why would it? An entrepreneur has more work motivation than the State. As a rule, an entrepreneur is a better manager. Yes, the State has more money, but if the entrepreneur in question hasn't wanted to put more of his own money into this factory (because he considers it unprofitable), why would the State want to? The more money the State puts in, the greater the loss. But the State budget is a national pocket; in other words, if someone takes money from it and throws it into a black hole like this fellow's factory, there may not be enough State money left to pay someone else's salary, and yet another fellow will have to pay more in taxes. What for? To satisfy someone's ambitions? Because someone is stupid? Perhaps because someone wishes to retain control over the tap that, in turn, controls the "budgetary injections"?

Some of these State people say that a particular company or product promotes national security. Maybe. But then what we have to do is to finance the State order, and the potential bankrupt will get out of debt on his own. They say that there is social tension among the factory's thousands of employees. This is also possible. But then what must be done is to finance skill conversion and job-placement programs. This would be much less expensive than keeping a factory going that produces something that nobody wants to buy. The money is better off invested in developing new companies that not only will yield competitive products and create new jobs, but will also pay taxes as they should.

CHAPTER V

SAME STRATEGY, NEW TACTICS: 1996

Projected income from privatization for 1996 was set at 12 trillion rubles. The genesis of this notorious figure was not so much economic as it was linked, on the one hand, to the political situation in Russia, and, on the other, to the history of our relations with the International Monetary Fund and the problem of obtaining credits.

The political situation was sticky. Anticipating problems in dealing with the new Duma, the Government decided to boost the privatization figures in the draft budget. This way, they could later say that the large scale of privatization is due to budgetary demands (which by then would have been approved by the Duma!).

If we analyze the merits of this ruse, we can see that even though there was a certain logic to it, on the whole it should have raised serious doubts. It should have been noted that the projected income from privatization was based on an analysis of the securities market in the fall of 1994, when the market was on the rise and experts were optimistic about its future. But, as we remember all too well, after that fall the market collapsed, and in 1995 we entered a disheartening stage (largely of the Government's own making). On the one hand, there were these ambitious budget projections, approved by the Duma at the suggestion of the Government itself; on the other, demand on the market was weak (partly due to Vladimir Polevanov's pronouncements). Finally, there was a limitation on the resources available to meet the projection, resulting from the Duma's success banning the sale of shares of oil companies. (Of course, we got out of that trap with the pledge auctions, as described in Chapter IV, which produced some 5 trillion rubles for the federal Government, saved the reputation of privatization, and thwarted the Duma's plan to reverse course.)

As for relations with the IMF and their role in the drafting of the budget, there was a very specific problem. In other countries, privatization income is not a budgetary item, but is aimed at patching the budget deficit. IMF experts repeatedly proposed that the Government of the Russian Federation change the budgetary classification and remove privatization receipts from budget revenue, transferring them to reducing the deficit. The Duma (represented by Mikhail Zadornov and Sergey Glazyev) understood the IMF's position. However, for all the apparent soundness of this position, it had one serious flaw. If 12 trillion rubles were taken from the budget revenues, then the deficit would grow by that amount, exceeding the limits set by the IMF. The IMF suggested reducing the deficit by raising revenues from other sources, but the Government knew well that no such sources existed. The seemingly "pro-Western" position of the Duma was, in fact, an attempt to wreck the planned agreement with the IMF.

The Government did not fall into the Duma's trap, and did not increase the deficit. As a result, agreements were signed with the IMF for the granting of credit.

Accordingly, the budget projection of receipts from privatization in 1996 was set purely arbitrarily, i.e., as the difference between actual receipts and the budget deficit set by the IMF. In practice, it was done in the following way: one took the budget target for 1995, 8.7 trillion rubles, and multiplied this figure by the 1996 deflation index. Thus 11.7 trillion rubles were obtained.

Though the GKI perfectly realized the absurdity of this figure, on April 10, 1995, we had to send the Ministry of the Economy a report elaborating privatization receipts of 11.7 trillion rubles; the target budget was based on this very figure. Later, on September 15, when it became absolutely clear that the budget target on privatization in 1995 was too high as well, the GKI sent the Committee for Budget, Taxation, Banks, and Finance of the State Duma a letter elaborating receipts for 1996 of 5.6 trillion rubles. However, by this time the Government had already submitted a draft budget with the figure of 11.7 trillion rubles in privatization receipts to the Duma for review. Consequently, at the Government's order, the GKI was obliged to send a new letter to the Duma (revoking the previous one) where it again substantiated the grossly inflated figure of 11.7 trillion. With what great ardor we were trying to prove to our opponents that privatization could bring profit; I myself have always been sure that wherever privatization takes place in the world, it is conducted for reasons other than pure profit.

In any event, the 11.7 trillion ruble target of receipts from privatization remained in the 1996 budget, and we had to start seriously thinking of what strategy to adopt. In my view, two strategies were possible.

The first was to submit a proposal to the Duma to adjust the budget's privatization income from 11.7 trillion rubles down to 5.6 trillion rubles. This strategy, with some political reservations, had certain pragmatic advantages. The credit accords with the IMF were already signed, and the IMF would hardly cancel them just because of a deficit increase of only 6.1 trillion rubles—less than 0.5% of GNP.

The other plan was to meet the budget projection, in a novel way. We could transfer stock from federal ownership to regional, thus shifting 2.6 trillion rubles from federal debt to regional budgets. Then, we would carry out regional privatization plans to the tune of 1.1 trillion rubles, e.g., selling Svyazinvest for 1.9 trillion rubles (with the proceeds going to the federal budget). This would make up the necessary 5.6 trillion rubles.

The second strategy entailed meeting the budget projections rather than adjusting them. Although risky, it was doable. This entailed a transfer of stock from federal to regional ownership, thus shifting 4 trillion rubles from the federal debt to regional budgets. It was more difficult, since it involved the financing of "protected" items of local budgets, but it was not impossible. We needed to coordinate the actions of the GKI and the Ministry of Finance, which had to clamp down on the provinces, somewhat undercutting the financing of regional budgets by offering them shares instead of money, should the local administrations complain.

The latter plan, difficult to carry out, also involved several other steps. We had to sell shares pledged back in 1995 in the amount of half a trillion rubles after September 1, 1996, as well as shares of regional oil companies (Vostochnaya Oil Company, Tyumenskaya Oil Company, ONAKO, SIBUR), for some half a

trillion rubles, and remaining blocks of shares of large oil companies such as SIDANKO and Rosneft, of Unified Energy Systems
(EES), Rosgosstrakh, and of the St. Petersburg Seaport.

The dubiousness of this scheme did not stem from lack of
demand for these stocks; the difficulty was that the last thing the
branch ministries and administrators wanted was to see these
companies escape State control (in fact, *their* control). Management was dead-set against these measures, never mind that these
ministries and departments were poor managers. The political
situation, too, was far from favorable to investors, including foreign ones.

If the political and economic situation in the country in early
1996 was not conducive to privatization, part of the fault may lie
with us. We had not done well in public relations, and failed to
explain to the public the advantages of privatization.

Derivatives and convertible bonds used in the sale of LUKoil,
the release of American deposit receipts (ADR) of Mosenergo,
and pledge auctions all attracted more resources than the cash
auctions. At the same time, however, we felt that the momentum
of voucher privatization was almost exhausted, and we needed a
new format.

There were objective domestic political reasons why
privatization entered a lull just then. For one thing, its future was
directly linked to the winner of the Presidential elections in June.
I was convinced that we had to regroup and spend the first half of
1996 defending our progress thus far, including the finalization
of the securities market and the development of new tools for the
fall, when world markets would revive. There was no need to gal-
lop ahead into the bright future of privatization, just as there is
none now. Therefore, I preferred the former option of the two we
faced.

If the Presidential election were to turn out in favor of privatization, we would wait for an upturn in economic activity and higher demand on the securities market in September and October (we calculated that the volume of investments would reach $5 to $6 billion, even exceeding the 1994–95 indicators). With this scenario, we could expect growth in the private sector. We calculated that investment demand would fall most heavily on second-issue shares, which meant an immediate impact on production volume.

On the other hand, should the privatization opponents win and move the country to the left, we would expect total stagnation of the securities market. Even a few spectacular cases of nationalization could scare off potential investors. I doubted anyone would wish to take such risks. Everyone would lose out: the national economy, the shareholders (of whom there were 40 million at that time), and the State. There had already been a precedent for this, when, in the fall of 1994, every employee of Norilsky Nickel received shares by closed subscription. As a result of capitalization, the tab came to 12 million rubles (at a rate of about 1,000 rubles to the dollar). Later, as a result of highly publicized attempts to "review the results of privatization," the Norilsky Nickel stock steadily declined; in February 1996, one worker's share was worth only 4 million rubles at a rate of 4,500 rubles to the dollar. Thus, as a result of the criticism of privatization, each worker lost 11 of the 12 million rubles he or she owned.

A market survey conducted by the GKI revealed that while investment demand in the first half of 1996 could be estimated at two to four trillion rubles, foreign investment represented only half a billion rubles. Of the 150 foreign investors with whom the GKI closely cooperated by this time, only two were prepared to risk their capital before the Presidential elections. This was the result of the constant criticism leveled against privatization. This campaign, which amounted to criticism for its own sake, was launched in December 1995 and January 1996 by politicians who rejected the idea of private ownership outright and preached State ownership of major industries. The harm this did to the privatization process was immeasurable. As their main reason for refusing to invest their capital in the first half of 1996, 40.5% of potential investors mentioned the instability of the political situation, while 41.12% cited the lack of legal guarantees for investments. Had Gennady Zyuganov won the election, he would not have even had to ban privatization. It would have died on its own.

ALEXANDER KAZAKOV, MASTER OF DEFENSE

But a real assault on privatization was still to come, after the Duma elections. A commission was formed to analyze privatization results and to find culprits to blame for any negative consequences. Yeltsin could not afford to defend us too actively, as the election campaign was already under way and his consultants advised him to steer away from an unpopular issue like privatization. I disagreed, but perhaps they were right. Perhaps this was the right tactic. After all, they had to play it safe and not take risks.

Chubais was dismissed; Belyaev was dispatched to the Duma. Our team lost both a leader and a protector. It took us a long time to decide who should become the new Chairman of the State Property Committee. We were more interested in our goal than in the person of a would-be President. Since it was clearly impossible to keep privatizing in the same dynamic, aggressive way as before, we had to focus on mounting a solid defense. We were under attack from all directions: the Public Prosecutor's Office, the State Audit Office, the President's Control Department, the Ministry of Finance's Accounts, and the Cash Department. We felt besieged. No one seemed to want to defend privatization. We saw only one person capable of defending us: Alexandr Kazakov.

Prior to being appointed Chairman of the State Property Committee in January 1996, Kazakov had already worked in the GKI between 1992 and 1994, first as Chief of the Department for Supervision of Territorial Property Committees and Agencies, then as the Committee's Vice Chairman. In his very first statement as Chairman, he stressed that the companies would be privatized on a company-by-company basis. From the outset he immediately tried to distance himself firmly but tactfully from the mistakes and blunders of earlier stages of privatization. He declared that it was necessary to avoid the "previous obsession with the pace of privatization."

Kazakov gradually aligned the position of the GKI with that of the Parliament, branch ministries, and regional elites. He appealed for a cap on privatizations from above and for the transfer of more powers to the regions. I feel that Alexandr Kazakov clearly understood that preserving privatization as a whole required concessions and tradeoffs, at least until June 1996. I think that this is why he unhesitatingly agreed to participate in the work of the Duma commission that was analyzing privatization results. His words in addressing the deputies ("we are the executive and will do what you tell us") became a catch-phrase.

Kazakov relied on three factors: development of a securities market, defense of shareholders' rights, and efficient management of State property. The new GKI chairman also thought it was fairly impossible to achieve the projected privatization income, but he resigned himself to the necessity of trying to implement it. First, it was a separate article of the Budget Law. Second, the President and the Prime Minister had ordered the GKI to collect receipts in the planned amounts. Third, the State Duma never made any changes to this item in the budget. As in 1995, we were again required to make "unorthodox decisions." It is true that Kazakov soon doubted there was an effective method of achieving this objective and started asking Duma deputies rhetorical questions like, "Where do you expect me to find the 12.7 trillion rubles planned in the budget?"

To me, the dismissal of Anatoly Filatov from the position of Director General of Norilsky Nickel in April 1996 was a good example of Alexandr Kazakov's work as Chairman of the State Property Committee. Unfortunately, we had not found common language with Filatov, whose actions were inconsistent and unpredictable. On April 5, Filatov sent Chernomyrdin and Soskovets a letter in which he proposed that the government either fire him and dissolve the board of directors of Norilsky Nickel (of which he was the head) or keep the existing board and limit the rights won in the pledge auction at the end of 1995. Up until that moment, the Government had been unsure if it favored the old management, bankers, and others. In April of 1996, however, it finally came out on the side of the private investors. Filatov was dismissed, and I must give Kazakov credit. This Governmental decision was due almost exclusively to his tenacity.

THE STATE AUDIT OFFICE VS. KOKH AND MOSTOVOY

Despite all our fears on the eve of the June Presidential elections, Yeltsin won. Had the outcome been different and Communist leader Gennady Zyuganov the winner, not only would the GKI have been liquidated, but I myself would not have gotten away with a mere dismissal. In anticipation of such a scenario, shortly before the elections the State Audit Office proposed bringing a criminal action against me, charging me with inefficiency and abuse of power in the course of privatization.

In the spring of 1996, acting on the Duma's instructions, the State Audit Office conducted a two-month audit of the GKI, the RFFI, and the Federal Insolvency and Bankruptcy Office. It concluded that the pledge auctions had violated the law. As an example, they claimed that the GKI instructions on conducting pledge auctions were not registered at the Ministry of Justice. In truth, we had an official letter from that ministry stating that these instructions "are not statutory in nature and do not need to be registered with the State authorities." The State Audit Office also felt I did not have the right to represent major Russian companies there.

Kazakov, our Chairman, stated our basic agreement with the findings of the State Audit Office, though he didn't deal with the content of their main report. For their part, the State Audit Office published two documents. The first of them, the findings proper, contained eight dry businesslike statements, devoid of personal attacks. The second, The Report of the State Audit Office, contained a list of some 150 allegations against privatization in general, the GKI, myself, and Petr Mostovoy. Kazakov added that he found it unlikely that we could have deliberately exceeded our authority or misused it. "I feel that this is a matter of individual opinion," he said, "and can hardly become a basis for a court decision." The arguments used by the State Audit Office in its attempts to prove the illegality of pledge auctions had already been heard and rejected during the arbitration examination following the claim of Norilsky Nickel. At the same time, according to Anatoly Chubais, "extraordinary pressure was exerted on the General Prosecutor's office to institute criminal proceedings" against me and Mostovoy.

It came to the point where in April we had been informed that I was no longer entitled to a Government dacha (apartment). Since I was urgently needed by the Kazakhstan ambassador, I was given one day to pack my belongings. We did not manage to meet that deadline, and in our absence someone simply collected and removed our belongings. I could not find who instigated or executed this hostile act. The Head of the President's Administration, Pavel Borodin, kept assuring me that I would have no problems and that I could live in the dacha for "as long as I liked." I have felt bitter about State housing ever since, and do not use their facilities any more.

I should mention that the Duma deputies and the State Audit Office have always shown an excessive degree of interest in me. Of course, it wasn't surprising, since I was the one who had carried out the most important privatization auctions of the last years (they were actually carried out by RFFI, but under my direction). That was the reason the name of Kokh kept coming up in all the privatization scandals. Quite simply, the heightened interest came with the territory.

However, I have always been sure that none of these scandals was grounded in fact. My certainty is based on the Arbitration Board's rulings concerning privatization affairs. All our decisions, including ones concerning pledge auctions, confirm that we have never broken the law. Despite numerous appeals from the State Audit Office, the Prosecutor General's Office never found it possible to bring a criminal charge against me. There were people who for political, psychological, emotional or other reasons were displeased by what I was doing as Chairman of the State Property Committee. But there is not one bit of evidence that I have ever done anything illegal.

I now believe it was Kazakov, whom I now consider a close friend, who saved my hide at this point, plain and simple, from the Prosecutor's and the State Audit Offices. Had he not taken a clear and firm position on Mostovoy and myself, we would have been destroyed.

Attacks on privatization were voiced by the State Audit Office at a session the Government held on April 18, 1996, where I announced the results of privatization for 1995. Following the debate, Viktor Chernomyrdin thanked the GKI for its work, confirming that the results of privatization would not be reviewed and that my resignation was no longer on the agenda. And that put an end to these attacks.

As Chairman of the State Property Committee, Kazakov did an excellent job. Some generals are born for offense, some are perfect at defense; Kazakov was of the latter kind. He parried every blow, confronted every conflict, and befriended every potential adversary. In August 1996, he took a job in the President's Administration, and I was soon appointed Chairman of the State Property Committee. By then, one could hear only the slightest echoes of the political war of a few months ago. Before me I saw a space wide open for maneuver, and I used it to the fullest extent possible.

THE FIFTH CHAIRMAN OF THE STATE PROPERTY COMMITTEE

The elections did not turn out the way the Communists had planned, and within a few months of the election (September 12) I was appointed Chairman of the GKI.

As Chairman, I considered it my first priority to improve the internal structure of the new private sector and equity-market infrastructure. Another priority was to make businesses more open to view. On the volume side, I was happy with the size of the private sector at the moment. About 70% of all enterprises were now privatized. For a former Communist country, that number was astounding. Our private sector at that moment was already larger than that of Great Britain, and in this sense we could consider ourselves more of a capitalist country. That is why I considered the management of State property and the restructuring of industry a more important issue at that time than privatization.

The two objectives of privatization and improving the management of State property are like apples and oranges. They belong on two different levels. Privatization involves the short-term goal of generating income (and may become a short-term priority). The other goal is mid- or long-term; it would be a strange situation if the State had no property at all (though an ideal one, apart from obvious institutions like the Army). On the other hand, it is impractical to expect the management of State property to improve within a short time-frame.

PRIVATIZATION HAS A FISCAL NATURE

Five years of work in the GKI had turned me into a tough realist. This is how I came to the conclusion that privatization as such is only fiscal in nature. Practice has shown that it is impossible to take restructuring enterprises seriously as the second main objective of privatization. I did not (and still do not) see any efficient mechanism that can ensure effective control over the implementation of investment programs. Any attempt to analyze the state of implementation of investment programs of long-ago auctions shows that these programs worked out rather poorly. The problem was that, as a rule, successful bidders at investment auctions quickly succeed in finding a common language with managers. We have often faced situations in which a director did not want to show how the terms of the investment program were being fulfilled, and without his participation noncompliance was hard to detect. Even if all the investment payments have been officially made, tracing kickbacks is all but impossible. This is the main problem.

One of my favorite books is *My Past and My Thoughts,* by Alexander Herzen, the great 19th-century Russian writer and thinker. There is a remarkable episode in this book that illustrates this situation well. Herzen's first and most powerful impression of England was of a truly democratic country. Two tipsy lads come out of the pub and start a brawl. The initial reaction in Russia, France, Italy, or most anywhere would be to call a policeman to separate them and mete out appropriate punishment. But here the two lads go on fighting and the policeman just looks on. People come up to him and say: "Aren't you going to do anything? It is getting really ugly." The policeman replies: "Neither of them is calling for help; they are having fun. They are not disturbing anyone: they're just punching each other in the face." That's democracy. Provided no one complains, the authorities are not bound to intervene.

IMPROVING BOTH THE QUALITY OF MANAGEMENT AND THE EFFICIENT USE OF FEDERAL PROPERTY

Despite the fact that by 1996 the private sector of Russia's economy was fully operational, the State remained a full-fledged player and a powerful property owner. The basic forms of State property comprised single-form ownership of companies, blocks of shares in companies created during privatization, and federal real estate and State property abroad.

The main forms of management of State property, other than privatization and leasing, included participation in the management of joint-stock companies, transfer of shares into trusteeship, transfer of property into the authorized capital of joint-stock companies, and transfer of property to the economic control or day-to-day management of non-State entities. In 1996, I understood that privatization had reached a saturation point, and that we could no longer expect a substantial increase in the "privatization component" of income from operations involving State property. Under these conditions, the efficiency of State property management became a particularly important issue. To cite one example: The 1997 budget provides for the receipt of two and a half trillion rubles, part from leasing federal property and part in the form of dividends on blocks of shares in federal ownership.

MANAGEMENT OF STATE PROPERTY

In 1996, there were more than 30,000 State-owned companies and organizations in the Russian Federation, including 893 in the defense sector and 1,257 in the fuel-and-energy complex. Operating them and coordinating their activities was generally the task of federal executive authorities. Branch ministries and agencies had the right to incorporate the statutes of federal enterprises, fire and hire managers, and conclude, amend, and terminate contracts with these managers. The GKI's jurisdiction covered all legal measures involved in creating, restructuring, and liquidating federal enterprises, transferring federal property to full economic management, managing day-to-day operations, and leasing to legal entities on the basis of signed agreements. The GKI's jurisdiction in fact extended over every aspect of the proper use and protection of federal property.

Analysis of State management has shown that a number of branch ministries and agencies (e.g., the Ministry of Atomic Energy, the Ministry of Telecommunications) have created efficient management systems through detailed registration of existing State enterprises in regularly updated registers, and through regular verification of incorporation documents. Nevertheless, there is no doubt that the effectiveness of State enterprises lags behind that of private enterprises or companies with a partial State-owned stake.

No analysis was conducted of these enterprises, of the relationship between their output and the existing demand, or of possible redundancy. Therefore, there was no restructuring or liquidation of even the least efficient state enterprises.

It turned out that some enterprises operated without statutes and even without a license. There were cases where a director worked without a contract, even cases of self-liquidation by state enterprises that the branch ministries and agencies only heard about through sheer luck.

Properties managed by the enterprises themselves and owned by the State were practically outside the owner's sphere of influence. Working outside the independent supervision of management was virtually nonexistent. While constantly arguing against privatizing a number of enterprises, and for nationalizing them instead, the branch ministries and agencies nevertheless often invited the GKI to sell property of State enterprises that were excluded from privatization.

Some branch ministries and agencies believed that the best way of improving the situation of State enterprises was to have them run directly by the State, i.e., to transfer them to direct budget financing regardless of performance. The ministries and agencies drew up a list of 700 such enterprises that they felt should be converted into State-run enterprises, due to their insolvency.

It soon became patently obvious that leaders of most State enterprises were ill-prepared to operate in a market economy. There were many reasons for poor management standards. The main ones were the estrangement of the owner (the State) from control over the financial and economic activities of enterprises and their leaders, the nonsupervision of leaders by ministerial departments and administrations, the inability to make decisive personnel decisions concerning senior managers, and a lack of capable managers who could work in a market environment without budget resources. Such managers either push for full or partial privatization of their enterprises, or leave for the private sector.

We concluded that the existing system of State enterprise management was wholly ineffective and demanded crucial changes; the right to manage actually *prevented* the owner (the State) from managing its own property, as its role was limited to overseeing property transferred to economic management, and participating in profits.

We decided that by January 1, 1999, all federal single-form-ownership enterprises managed on an economic basis would be converted into companies with 100% State capital, or into State-run federal enterprises. Since all net earnings of a joint-stock company derived from State-owned shares must be reallocated to the budget, it had become obviously necessary to abolish the right of economic management and to convert most State enterprises into joint-stock companies. State-run federal enterprises must be created only when production cannot yield profits but is essential to State security. There are only a handful of such enterprises in the country. The federal budget clearly cannot bear the burden of 700 State-owned enterprises. This is precisely why we invited the Government to limit the number of federal-run enterprises in the country to 100–150.

During the transition period, it became necessary to regulate the mechanisms of managing State property transferred to economic management. We needed to clarify the owner's control over property transferred to the single-form State authority; to draft and adopt the main terms of transfer agreements from federal property to economic management; to have professional appraisers assess State property being transferred as collateral, for lease, or to authorized capital of commercial organizations (the absence of a law on valuation work does not prevent this); to audit major State enterprises with the participation of financial consultants; and to solve the problem of transferring lease-worthy property (not subject to privatization but belonging to privatized enterprises) to specially created State enterprises. The experience of developed countries (France, Italy) and countries whose economies are in transition (Brazil, Mexico, India) suggests creating vertically integrated industrial State structures that would manage State property under trusteeship. However, in creating such structures, steps must be taken to monitor compliance with antimonopoly legislation and to prevent, through collective responsibility, any unlawful estrangement of State assets.

In 1996, the Russian Federation owned 2,900 blocks of shares in joint-stock companies and other enterprises with mixed forms of ownership. In accordance with the Presidential Decree of the Russian Federation of May 11, 1995, federal ownership could comprise blocks of shares only in those companies that produced goods or services of strategic importance or essential for national security. The list of 2,700 companies established under the decree of September 1995 subsequently kept being extended (in 1996 alone, a dozen related Government acts were adopted).

Proportions of shares in federal property in the authorized capital of joint-stock companies were as follows: over 50%—286; 25% to 50%—1,037, below 25%—228; below 20%—303; "golden share"—1,351. The nominal value of federal blocks of shares was some seven trillion rubles, but the market value was estimated by independent experts at a quadrillion and a half rubles.

The State also controls its shares through the Institute of Representatives appointed by the decisions of the President, the Government, the GKI, and the RFFI. There were about 2,000 such representatives at this time. In the cases where making decisions and voting required approval by superiors, the GKI issued written directives to the State representative. These concerned such questions as the introduction of changes and additions to statutory documents, changes in the size of authorized capital, the appointment and election of specific persons to management and controlling bodies, the receipt of credits exceeding 10% of net assets, the sale and other estrangement of real estate and mortgaging, and the participation of companies in the creation of other enterprises (including the incorporation of affiliates) and financial-industrial groups (FPGs).

Having analyzed the work of State representatives, we discovered a number of serious flaws. Among them:

- Irregularities in State representatives' work in joint-stock companies, primarily on boards of directors; absence of branch ministries and agencies from appointments of

State representatives; accounting irregularities by State representatives or absence of accounting altogether.

- Absence of State representatives from active work in joint-stock companies on the pretext that they were limited in their rights to influence current activities.
- State representatives' violations of approval procedures concerning their activities on the part of supervising bodies, and violations of instructions issued, including instructions when voting.
- Low professional skills of many State representatives recruited from among State officials.

Despite the repeated proposals of the GKI, no procedures were elaborated for defining the general status of State representatives of various federal executive bodies, analogous to the procedures on such representatives in oil companies established in August 1994 by the joint decision of the GKI, the Ministry of Energy, and the GKAP (State Committee for Anti-Trust Policy). Finally, the very institution of State representatives as State civil servants contradicted the law, "On the Foundations of Civil Service in the Russian Federation," as was pointed out on many occasions by the General Prosecutor's Office.

I felt that there were two ways to improve the management of federal blocks of shares: (1) increase the liability of State representatives, while improving their efficiency; and (2) use various forms of outside management (e.g., trusteeship or hired managers). In my mind, both these directions could work equally well. Also, one should not examine the management system separately without first examining the object of said management, i.e., blocks of shares.

Apart from all that, the State's blocks of shares had to be optimized. I am convinced that this portfolio had to include blocks representing 75% of shares (when full control over the activity of a company was required) and controlling blocks representing 51% of shares. It seemed reasonable to convert blocking interests representing 25.5% of shares to "golden shares" and to sell blocks of shares of less than 25% when conditions were most favorable, and after compulsory presale preparation.

Upon analysis, we concluded that the strategic size of the State stock portfolio must come to 1,000 blocks of shares in joint-stock companies created during privatization. We were not afraid to admit that any greater amount would be too much for the State to handle effectively.

The GKI developed a plan of action aimed at defending the State as owner and shareholder, and at increasing the control of management of federally owned stock. In addition to improving procedures (norms and standards), we proposed that agreements be concluded with private professional managers who would represent the interests of the State in the management of companies with mixed forms of ownership, and that we "privatize" the control over federal blocks of shares by transferring them to the trusteeship management of commercial bodies. Given the proposal of the GKI on the radical reduction of the size of federal blocks of shares, the main purpose of trusteeship management became presale preparation (inducing the rise in value for stock in federal property, raising their liquidity, etc.).

A NEW STAGE IN THE MANAGEMENT OF STATE PROPERTY

It is plain to see why we started developing new ways of controlling State blocks of shares (pledging them or transferring them into trusteeship). It is no secret that the State is unable to exercise its rights and obligations as owner and shareholder fully. On the one hand, the State has never had the financial or other resources. On the other hand, it has always suffered a chronic shortage of skilled managers. Finally, acting through its bureaucracy, the State has inevitably proved weaker than other shareholders since its representatives lacked incentives. This affected policies of joint-stock companies in the areas of taxation, dividends, and payroll that often did not coincide with the interests of the State. This is why we needed radical changes in the system of State control over blocks of shares in federal property.

In 1996, we started working on a program with four main elements. We first proposed that a portion of the federal shares be transferred to management by private individuals (so-called nominees). Another portion would be kept under the management of State officials from branch ministries and agencies, but this time based on signed contracts. Third, certain blocks of shares would be transferred on a competitive basis to the trusteeship of major financial organizations (primarily Russian). Lastly, some of the shares would, as before, be used in the creation and development of financial-industrial groups.

At first we devised a mechanism for concluding agreements with nominees; then we moved on to a mechanism for transferring stock into trusteeship. The main aim of the trusteeship auctions was to transfer control over federal stock into the hands of more effective managers, thereby increasing the investment appeal of companies and the market value of the stock. It was proposed that the contests should also help draw income to the federal budget. This income would come, first, from selling trustee rights; second, from payment by the auction winner of a joint-stock company's indebtedness to the Government; third, from a reduction in State subsidies, tax privileges, and State investments; and finally, due to growing income in the form of dividends on shares and increase in share price, from an increase in the company's tax base.

Generally speaking, transfer of State blocks of shares into trusteeship had taken place earlier. But we felt it was necessary to make the process more open and competitive, and to provide clear criteria for determining winners. In particular, this referred to the price the winner was prepared to pay the State for the right to become a trustee manager of federal stock. (In my own personal view, stimulating the creation of financial-industrial groups could have been accomplished as well through the former system, whereby the transfer of the management of federal stocks to financial and industrial groups was not competitive and was free of charge.)

Even before the final draft of this plan came out, our opponents accused us of having designed a covert way to sell shares (the same accusation as had been leveled earlier in regard to pledge auctions). I categorically disagreed. Just like the winner of a pledge auction, the successful bidder did not become the owner of State stock, which remained State property. Even though a trustee received fairly broad powers, he was obliged to get the owner's (the State's) agreement on all important decisions. The State remained protected from the unwilling loss or reduction of its stock, from company closure or property transfer; before approving a profit-and-loss statement or voting on profit, the trustee was obliged to seek authorization from the State. Moreover, unlike the pledge scheme, there was not even a theoretical provision allowing the trustee ever to sell the stock. And income from these trusteeship contests was to be entered in the federal budget as income from the management of federal property, not as privatization income.

There were other differences as well between trusteeship and pledge auctions. Unlike pledge auctions, in trusteeship auctions the State received money immediately, with no other obligations on its part; trusteeship was conferred for a period of three years. The motivation for potential participants in the contest would be remuneration—to the tune of 30% of the dividends on shares they would manage during the three-year period—as well as the possibility of extending the agreement for a further period, without additional payment.

These auctions were also organized differently. For example, we suggested that the advance be raised considerably, to as much as 25% of the initial pledge (at pledge auctions the advance was only 3%, which did not really guarantee that participants' attitudes toward the auction requirements would be responsible). All sorts of additional requirements for participation in the auctions were stipulated in detail. These might include making investments, settling debts to the budget, or depositing as much as 100% of the bid. The auction organizers announced these requirements beforehand. We even added one requirement omitted during the "pledge epic": that participants submit to a preliminary check by the State Anti-Monopoly Committee in order to ensure compliance with antimonopoly laws. Unlike pledge auctions, these auctions were not open to the individuals and companies whose stock was being sold. The Committee also reserved the right to limit the participation of foreign companies in certain lots. In the future, the Committee itself (including a representative of the Ministry of Economy) was supposed to receive and register applications, analyze documents, and authorize the participation of applicants.

In addition, the advance payments had to be paid to GKI's account at a bank chosen by the Government in agreement with the Central Bank. A potential participant in a trustee auction had to present his balance sheet for the last fiscal year, certified by the tax authorities. Applying banks had to show resources of no less than 50% of the starting price. Other applicants had to prove possession of clear assets totaling no less than 50% of the starting price; yet others had to prove they held assets equal to the starting price of the lot and owed no taxes to budgets at any level. We hoped that this would keep shady, fly-by-night companies away from the auctions. Moreover, from that time on a participating bank was under no obligation to produce a guarantee from another bank.

A lot of the noise and litigation concerning the results of pledge auctions had stemmed from the sheer quantity, on the one hand, and bidders' carelessness, on the other. In order to avoid future conflicts, we proposed that now organizers would have up to seven days to examine documents submitted for a trustee management auction; they would also be required to announce the admission or rejection of a participant no less than three days in advance of the contest, not on the same day.

The GKI's position (and mine) was that a trustee manager whose main goal was to increase the company's productivity had to be selected on the basis of his personal involvement, so that his private interests coincided with those of the State. It would be possible to link his commission to the profits, to budget income, or to the volume of products sold and paid for.

174

Since the President's decree on trustee management, prepared by us, was supposed to be based on the auction principle, none of the winners would be known beforehand. The particular branch ministry and its departments would automatically entitled to that position of trustee manager, especially since it would be one of the ministry's functions to supervise it.

Our approach to the problem of transferring shares to trustee management seemed to me more appropriate than the alternative proposed by the Ministry of Industry and supported by branch ministries and departments. They simply requested the right to manage the block of shares in question, and believed this to be a more effective form of share management. This would, however, be worse than the previous situation, when 90% of the State representatives in the joint-stock companies were functionaries of the branch departments, and were at least somewhat answerable to the GKI. Now the proposals brought up by branch ministries and agencies focused on gaining the vote on fixed blocks of shares independently, without GKI's previous agreement.

I was surprised that these people did not understand the downside of their own proposals, most importantly the splitting of management functions into parts. Participation of at least two federal bodies of executive power (the GKI and a branch ministry) in managing and controlling the State block of shares could certainly lead to imperfect control of this process or, in fact, no effective control at all.

The division of control between property and day-to-day management does not seem justifiable even now. And the experience of developed industrial countries repudiates a sector approach to management. As a rule, between ten and fifteen ministries and administrations with wide areas of competence operate in such countries. (Of course, in some places things work differently: in

Somalia, there is a Ministry of Coffee and a Ministry of Tea. But this is an amusing ethnographic detail, not a practice worth emulating.)

The story of that Presidential decree on trustee management had an unexpected ending. Its announcement in the fall of 1996 was immediately followed by a statement that the decree had been "neutered," as it actually concerned only a few coal-mining companies. I was personally accused of "neutering" it, allegedly to please the bankers, who, by the end of 1995, had received a block of State shares as a guarantee. This scenario sounds plausible only if you are unaware of one small but very important detail. The idea of trustee management came from the World Bank, which demanded that we create just such a mechanism for coal-mining stocks, as a prerequisite for granting coal credits to Russia. Indeed, the decree was only *supposed* to affect the coal industry, as we had asked. By no means did we want to use this mechanism on a broader scale.

Frankly, I am not much of a believer in trustee management, and will never be, especially trustee management of State shares. Compared to a private owner, a trustee manager has far less incentive to perform productively.

PRIVATIZATION STRATEGY IN 1996 As we continued our work into 1996, we increasingly understood that we were always working in two different directions at once, hoping they would coincide as often as possible:

The first direction reflected our perennial need for cash yield for the Government, our need, you might say, to justify privatizing the Russian economy by showing our countrymen that we could keep turning it upside down and shaking trillions of rubles out of it and into the wide-mouthed basket of the federal budget. This had not changed very much, except that after seeing us sweat bricks to make history by putting together almost 9 trillion, the Duma saw nothing remarkable in writing a *12-trillion-ruble* goal for privatization income into the 1996 Budget Law.

The second direction was about how we wanted our methods of preparing enterprises to go on the capital market to *change*. We had been guilty at times of a kind of slapdash marketing to investors; too much more of that and we would end up with disappointing results, a lot of private companies with not enough capital to really change their functioning, and a level of attractiveness so low as to be unlikely to lure any new help.

But the Svyazinvest sale had almost gone through, and we felt good about how that sale had been prepared. So we decided to see our 1996 program as a series of highly individual projects, in which we would study the specific nature of each project and provide for substantial presale preparation. We would be moving away from mass privatization to the privatization of "targeted projects," a transition from the extensive to the intensive.

What is privatization based on "individual projects"? And, more specifically, what constitutes good "presale preparation"? An individual or targeted project, as we understood it, is a series of steps aimed at privatizing federal property of special importance for the country, a region, or sector of the economy; this includes presale preparation of the property with the participation of independent financial consultants.

The first step in presale preparation was always to complete the consolidation of blocks of shares in authorized capital, which would lead to stronger vertical integration and improved management.

In selling shares through commercial auctions we decided always to make use of the services of a financial consultant, who was to be selected on a competitive basis and whose tasks were numerous and well defined. Financial consultants had been used before, but now they became a permanent fixture of our operations. These tasks would always include (1) helping to organize the auction, (2) attracting bidders, and (3) preparing information (more and more the heart of presale preparation—not only to trumpet the great opportunities but to promote among the new leaders in industry the awareness that the old pigs-in-pokes were going to get a little more modern public exposure) as called for in the contract they would always sign with us.

That contract would also always stipulate (4) that the consultant act as underwriter for the shares sold under the terms of the auction, and at a price not lower than the starting price, and would also (5) take responsibility for the final allocation of shares on a competitive basis among entities entitled to participate as investment houses; the underwriter might also (6) act as broker in the sale of bonds convertible to ordinary shares of joint-stock companies and receive the commission, possibly with the participation of other investment brokers who would ensure that shares were sold on international securities markets; and might (7) transfer shares to trusteeship management and (8) issue convertible bonds and derivatives. The underwriter-consultant would receive no commissions if the sales failed; thus, there was risk involved, but also great incentive to prepare the sales well and make them successful.

Decisions about implementing the financial consultant's recommendations would be made by a commission consisting of representatives of relevant ministries and departments, whose composition would be approved by the State Property Committee.

One clear example of a consultant's recommendation was the suggestion, in 1995, to organize a sale of convertible bonds of the LUKoil company.

By saying "an individual privatization project" we didn't mean using a special privatization *method*: the list of existing methods was clearly defined in the Privatization Law. The specific nature of a project lay in its *preparation*: evaluation of the financial situation of the company and of various restructuring possibilities, and the choosing of optimal methods and times for sales.

We had the Russian Marketing Association conduct a special survey in order to obtain information on the actual demand of Russian and foreign investors for shares, convertible bonds, and pledged stocks or stocks transferred to trusteeship management.

Four target segments of potential investors were identified: major commercial banks, investment houses (mutual funds) most active on the securities market (members of the Russian Professional Association of Securities Market Participants), foreign industrial and financial firms represented in Russia, and finally, those segments of the population that had by now accumulated enough personal wealth to think about investing.

In designing the survey, they picked shares in federal ownership of 13 of the largest enterprises being considered for "individual project" status—Gazprom; the oil companies Rosneft, SIDANKO, Sibneft, Eastern (Vostochnaya) Oil, Tyumen Oil, ONAKO, NORSIoil, and Unified Energy Systems (EES) of Russia; Svyazinvest; the Novosibirsk Electrode Plant; the St. Petersburg Seaport; Rossgosstrakh—as well as shares of other companies being privatized in leading economy sectors.

According to the survey, the total investment potential of all categories of investors in the securities of these 13 largest enterprises totaled 8.9 trillion rubles, assuming an inflation rate of 1%–2%; 8 trillion rubles at an inflation rate of 3%–5%; and 2.3 trillion rubles at an inflation rate of more than 5% per month. The investment potential of the shares of other companies undergoing privatization at the indicated inflation rates amounted to 3.3 trillion rubles, 3.3 trillion rubles, and 2.9 trillion rubles, respectively. With a rise of inflation for 1996 predicted from 1%–2% per month to 3%–5%, the total investment potential dropped by 5.9%, at an inflation rate of more than 5%, it went down 2.3 times. Given that there was already 4.2% monthly inflation in January 1996, we anticipated an investment response corresponding to a 3%–5% per month level.

The survey indicated that the main demand was for Gazprom shares (4.6 trillion rubles, or 55.7% of total demand for securities) and those of Rossgosstrakh (1.3 trillion rubles, or 15.2%). Aggregate demand for the oil companies' shares (mainly Rosneft and Sibneft) amounted to about one trillion rubles, or 11.9% of the total demand for securities of the 13. The aggregate demand of individuals for shares of the 13 largest enterprises being privatized amounted to 858 billion rubles.

Most people were ready to participate in specialized cash auctions; we had 1,000 points of sale all across Russia, usually in bank branches. But we felt this was not enough, that it was still too strange and inconvenient a step for them. It would have been easier if they could have placed orders at branches of the Russian Savings Bank, of which there are many, many thousands in Russia—far more than of any other bank; but they were not in our system. The market survey showed that if they could place their bids at these branches, they were ready to buy. We approached the top people at that bank and told them that we would like to sell stock at their branches and give them a commission, but the percentage they demanded was too high for us—something on the order of 10%. We decided we couldn't afford to take the step.

The purchase of stocks is always a complicated process, but it is particularly complicated in Russia. The major options include (1) buying stock in Russia offered for rubles: to do this, foreign investors (or Russians holding dollars) have to buy rubles first; register the stock in Russia, subject to all relevant Russian laws; and deposit the certificates with a custodian (it is not allowed to take the physical paper out of the country); and (2) the ADR (American Deposit Receipts) system, which offers an additional level of assurance that makes the sale more attractive: a bidder can buy from an American bank that has established a corresponding relationship with the Russian bank holding the shares for the Government, and pay in dollars; register the shares with the American bank; be subject only to U.S. law; and benefit from guarantees provided by the American bank.

The results of the marketing study conducted allowed us to conclude that we could properly plan sales that would bring significant income to the budget only for the first half of 1996. The reason was clear, since everyone knew that there was simply no telling what kind of system we would be living under a year hence. The Presidential elections were soon to take place, in June and July; the reader will recall that the Communists had just won in the Parliamentary elections. And it was impossible to say how things would change if the Communists won the upcoming contest; one almost preferred not to think about it, but change there would be, and the atmosphere was charged with doubt like a great cloud hanging in the air everywhere. People assumed significant renationalization, of that there could be no doubt—there had to be. One could easily imagine stocks losing much of their value.

Among the sales we did feel confident enough to plan were a 25%-plus-1 share of Svyazinvest and 15% of Rosneft in specialized cash auctions. Others included 6,633 blocks of shares in 4,589 joint-stock companies, of which 1,551 would be offering shares for the first time.

As time went on, we found we were also more and more involved in coordinating our privatization scheduling needs with a growing movement among the regional administrations also to become involved in privatization activities. The regional administrators were peppering us with requests for federal property in their regions and blocks of shares in enterprises in their regions to be transferred to their control and disposition in terms of timing, manner of sale, etc. In the Presidential Decree No. 292, of February 27, 1996, "On Transfer of Federally Owned Shares in Companies Formed During Privatization to Regional Authorities," a balance was worked out between the traditional aid sent to the regions from the center and privatization proceeds; Moscow was not always going to let them have both, but would want to post the value of transferred shares to the mutual settlements accounts between the governmental levels.

I had been trying to find new ways to maximize revenue in the first half of 1996, and I gave a lot of thought to these interrelationships, trying to understand them better. I saw that in the Russian federal structure of 88 entities, each of the regions has its budget and property—which is *not* federal property—and in addition would ask the federal Government very often to transfer to their control federal blocks of shares in regional enterprises. At the same time, the federal budget always had a special clause about payments to the regions under headings such as disaster relief and emergency aid; their own deficits tended to be covered by these payments. And the following idea struck me: give them a choice between our shares and those payments. When the shares were sold, the portion of the proceeds due us could be posted to the payments account, a relief to the federal budget. This was the idea embodied in Decree No. 292. It wasn't too surprising, though, when they continued to try to keep receiving both the shares and the payments!

One aspect of this perennial ambiguity was built into our system of regional property management. The federal Government always had representatives in every regional entity who were in charge of managing federal property. Administratively, however, such officials always reported to the regional governor and were under his jurisdiction. In 1996, when we gave the regions the option of benefiting from the sale of federal property, some tried to use this administrative control to block sales when they didn't like the prices; however, in 54 out of 88 regions, the sales went through.

One consequence of all this is that the Government—ourselves—now had the added task of compiling lists of company shares to be possibly transferred to the federation entities as well as possible transfer procedures, and to evaluate all of them. The value of transferred shares had to be no lower than the market value of similar shares. Allow me to emphasize that these transfers did not damage the country's strategic interests, because the list in question could not include shares of companies figuring in the Russian Federation Government Act No. 949 of September 18, 1995, the "List of Privatized Companies Whose Production (Goods or Services) Is of Strategic Importance for National Security and Whose Federally Held Stock Is Not Subject to Be Sold Ahead of Schedule."

On the whole, we expected to take in 6.266 trillion rubles from privatization in 1996. Federal income for the year would be distributed as follows: sale of Svyazinvest stock, 1.8 trillion rubles; Rosneft stock, 0.5 trillion rubles; scheduled sales, 0.685 trillion rubles; real estate sales, 0.281 trillion rubles, including the sale of the land, which would yield 0.072 trillion rubles; value of the shares transferred to the regions, to be posted as privatization income, 2–3 trillion rubles. Besides these sources, 217 billion rubles would arrive as income from assets in federal ownership.

On the basis of these calculations, we suggested that the budget projection should be corrected, because the sale methods defined by the existing legislation had already been exhausted and new ones could only be introduced by means of submitting to the Duma a draft of the State privatization program. Apart from that, the draft of a Presidential decree concerning the procedure of transfer into trusteeship management of shares in federal property was finally ready, providing that the winners of trustee auctions would supply the federal budget with guaranteed income. Actually, as we saw above, this Presidential decree on trusteeship management only referred to coal mining; it was never really implemented.

We were preoccupied with yet a different ambiguity, that between absorbing the rubles invested in our forthcoming sales of shares and the governmental effort to reduce inflation, stabilize the ruble, and work toward a more stable dollar-ruble relationship. Say we expected to sell $100 million worth of shares in rubles in 5–6 months, We projected the dollar-ruble ratio for each of the next few months. When in the middle of this process the government introduced the "currency corridor," i.e., a particular limited range for fluctuation of the ratio, this in a way knocked out many Russian investors from participating in forthcoming sales; they were holding dollars, and suddenly both the ruble and the stock being offered for rubles were more expensive.

But I believe it was only the uncoordinated suddenness on the part of the Central Bank that hurt the sales, not the idea of a currency corridor.

In general, I have come to have reservations about these constant budget projections. The present Government still calculates partial coverage of the budget from privatization, but I wonder now if it makes sense. Let's consider the typical budget bill, include a planned ("projected") deficit that it specifies will be covered by Treasury bonds and the proceeds of privatization—complete with numbers.

What is the reaction of the investor to this? Thanks to this legislation, he knows just how much money—and by when—the State will be under intense pressure to raise a few months hence. The State will be trying to sell certain properties to reach the figure, and he also knows that the pressure will grow the longer he waits. So he waits; inevitably, the price comes down, just as he has planned. I believe the Government should be free to sell when it knows that it's going to get a good price, that it should be allowed to be more clever than the way things are now. As these matters transpire currently, Government as a player in the market commits itself to a weak position—and everyone knows it, because the budget bill is public and the numbers are there for all to see. They come and say, "Sell that to me for $10!" and the Government tells them the price is $20. They say, "We know—by December you'll sell it for $10!!" because they understand the pressure created by the budget bill.

The first stage needed such a structure; there is certainly no doubt about that. But now such regulations do not contribute to the formation of a market; they only detract from it. This stage should provide the utmost profit from selling the property, and holding to this purpose first and foremost demands that no Government action be tied to a fulfillment plan.

Let me add parenthetically that the size of the assignment can change the nature of the dynamic. In the 1997 budget, the target set was 8 trillion. Nowadays this is not that great a sum—approximately 3% of the budget—an easy target, covered by selling two or three properties—and for once we were operating without pressure, because the target happened to be an easy one. What happened? We took in *17 trillion*—and I insist that had we had the kind of pressure we had before, we would never have been so successful!

FOR NEW TIMES, A NEW PRIVATIZATION PROGRAM: 1996

In 1996, our Committee (the GKI) drafted a federal bill entitled "Main Principles for the State Program Privatizing State and Municipal Enterprises in the Russian Federation." In general, we did our best to expand the range of methods of stock sale, reduce the privileges granted to employee groups, and elaborate procedures for real estate sales, while maintaining continuity with earlier privatization programs.

The proposed draft was a logical offshoot of privatization. At the same time, it took into consideration new legal instruments such as the new Civil Code of the Russian Federation and laws like "On Joint-Stock Companies and on General Principles of Organizing Local Self-Government in the Russian Federation." It also took into account the special nature of the Russian economy, in particular the evolving property structures of Russian companies resulting from privatization. This led us to shift priorities in privatization and basic attitudes in its implementation.

We hoped that the approval of the new program would be followed by changes in our work. The draft law defined the main aims of privatization as follows:

- improving the efficiency of the Russian economy in general, and of certain companies in particular
- bringing property-based relations in tune with the main directions of social and economic reforms in the country
- developing the real estate market
- increasing budget receipts and reducing budget expenses associated with the administration of the economy, unprofitable enterprises in particular
- protecting proprietors' interests
- attracting investments to production, including foreign investments

The draft also included a number of radically new proposals aimed at reaching the above objectives. We officially declared that we would no longer use number-based privatization indices— i.e., that we no longer cared about *how many* companies we converted—and that we would no longer grant privileges to employee groups. We expected this would actually increase the amount of stock offered at auctions and make it more attractive to investors, including foreign ones. This, in turn, would increase the income from privatization going into budgets at all levels. Experience had shown us that advantages granted to employee groups did not solve the social problems they were supposed to, they just hurt the economy, the company, and thus in the end the workers themselves.

We included in the draft a most important, historic section on privatizing real estate, for this issue remained one of the top priorities of our economic policy. Merely defining the problem in logical and coherent terms felt like an achievement, and our capacity to do this was in itself a result of the previous stages of privatization and of the establishment of new forms of management. Privatization of real estate would open vast opportunities for creating new economic conditions and mechanisms conducive to effective management.

Other features of the draft: It elaborated on the notion of "privatization income"; it extended and specified the conditions under which a decision can be taken to convert a structural subdivision of a company into a separate entity; finally, following repeated requests from ministries and agencies, we limited somewhat the number and kind of privatization transactions for which the parties had to supply a certificate detailing the source of their means.

In sum, 1996 was a year of gradual transition to privatization via individual projects and of improvement in the management of State property: it was also the year when privatization was finally recognized as much more than merely a method of drawing funds into the budget.

RESULTS OF CONVERSION OF STATE ENTERPRISES INTO JOINT-STOCK COMPANIES

All State and municipal enterprises whose capital assets book value exceeded 20 million rubles by January 1, 1994, were subject to conversion into open joint-stock companies. Companies excluded from privatization were used as State-run factories subject to sale to commercial groups with the participation of foreign investment.

As a result of the implementation of this requirement, the total number of enterprises privatized by January 1, 1997, went up to 126,793. This was 55% of the total number of State enterprises at the beginning of privatization. In 1996 alone, 4,997 enterprises were privatized; this was fewer by 51% than the number of enterprises privatized in the previous year. The same tendency could be observed by comparing the results of 1995 with those of 1994. (The breakdown of privatized enterprises by property forms is shown in Table 5.)

Thus, 1996 saw a steady downward trend in privatization. But this only meant that wholesale privatization was coming to an end; we were even starting to see a few industries and regions so intensely privatized as not to be capable of yielding any more such conversions.

For example, privatization was practically complete in sea and river transportation, where we had achieved a level of privatization comparable with that of developed industrial countries. Much progress was made in communications, where 95% of all enterprises were transformed into joint-stock companies, and in the fuel end energy industry (94%).

At the same time, different privatization methods began to change structurally. Territorial committees had finally started privatizing real estate, especially land. In 1996, the main methods of privatization were the transformation of State enterprises into joint-stock companies (22.4% of the total number of sales), the sale of real estate (22.9%), and the redemption of leased property (32.0%). The breakdown of privatized enterprises by privatization methods for 1993–96 is shown in Table 6.

By the end of 1996, the total number of joint-stock companies in our country rose to almost 30,000. As shown in Table 7, in 1996 as in 1995 the majority of joint-stock companies were

189

formed from enterprises that had been federal property. The trends in capital investment structures by property forms remained the same, due to continuing institutional reform and the decentralization of investment activity. In 1996, the private sector accounted for 74% of the total capital investments, compared to 69% in 1995.

STRATEGIES FOR DEPLOYING PRIVATIZATION METHODS

Let me mention again that privatization strategy in 1996 was forced to reflect the domestic political situation. It was a year of Presidential and gubernatorial elections, during which privatization was transformed from an economic notion into a political propaganda tool. This caused considerable fluctuation in share prices of privatized companies and anomalous sales patterns. Sales of shares were carried out in a highly irregular fashion. In the first six months, due to the political uncertainty caused by the elections, the demand for shares was not high. Therefore, the State Property Committee and the Russian Fund for Federal Property (RFFI) made a mutual decision not to offer shares for sale at securities auctions, given their low rate value. The bulk of State property sales fell on the last months of the year.

State property was privatized at monetary and specialized securities auctions on the basis of investment and commercial competitions, on a subscription basis, and through the Employees Incorporation Fund (FARP).

Also in 1996, our Committee transferred the shares of a total of 99 companies to the RFFI for sale, and the State Property Management Committees (KUGI) transferred privatization papers for 267 federal properties to the property funds.

Table 8 shows the main results of RFFI's sales of shares of enterprises being privatized. The largest auctions organized by RFFI in 1996 were the nationwide specialized auctions of 14.28% of Sibneft stock (134.4 billion rubles) and 7.86% of YUKOS stock (118.4 billion rubles), and the investment auctions of 16.07% of LUKoil stock (54.7 billion rubles and 800 billion rubles in investment) and 19% of the Sibneft shares (82.4 billion rubles and $45 million of investments).

FINANCIAL RESULTS OF 1996
As in 1995, income from privatization came in irregularly. During the first six months sales were made only in January and February. With the elections coming, conservative investors showed particular caution in the second quarter, even though it was during that period that the highest increase in equity prices took place on the secondary equity market. The peak in sales of the stock of privatized companies came in November and December.

The State Property Committee sent 1,374 billion rubles of income into the federal budget. Receipts from privatization came to slightly above a trillion (1,032.2 billion) rubles, which included the 203 billion in Federal debt transferred to regional budgets in accordance with Presidential Decree No. 292 of February 27, 1996, and 341.8 billion received from the management of federal assets.

Investments in the production capacity of joint-stock companies made by the winners of investment and commercial auctions exceeded 3.5 trillion rubles. An additional 310 billion rubles were transferred into the federal budget as settlement of overdue payments by these joint-stock companies.

Although the target figures on revenues from management of federal property were met, the projected input of 11.4 trillion rubles into the budget from privatization was not attained. This came as no surprise to us. We had discussed it openly when the 1996 budget was being passed.

Why were the target figures not met? In November, when our most pessimistic predictions regarding income from privatization had been confirmed, I sent a letter to Prime Minister Chernomyrdin in which I once again indicated that the authors of the 1996 budget had failed to take into account certain negative factors affecting investment, such as the elections and the resulting political atmosphere. Another factor neglected was the high profitability of GKO and other State securities, which were drawing off the bulk of available investment resources from the real sector (including company stocks) into the fiscal-speculative sector. Finally, I said, neglecting these factors had resulted in setting the budget figures at twice the amount they should have been.

Other reasons contributing to the failure to meet the figures included the suspension of sales of the stocks in a number of defense industry companies (for example, in the Nizhny Novgorod region alone this represented over twenty companies), following the Presidential Decree of April 13, 1996, "On Measures to Ensure Efficient State Control over the Privatization of Enterprises and Organizations in the Defense Sector." Another decree (No. 299) dealt with transfer of the blocks of shares from federal to regional ownership—a concession to the demands of regional administrations—and led to a suspension of the sales of stock of approximately 600 companies in 34 regions. Drafting the law that stipulated the above transfer was fraught with problems. The sale of the stocks of a group of coal mining companies was suspended due to the structural reconstruction of the sector (as per Presidential Decree No. 168, "On Measures to Further Improve the Structure of the Coal Industry in the Russian Federation," of February 9, 1996). The sale of blocks of shares of 157 other companies was also suspended following a resolution that had included them in the list of companies of strategic importance, whose shares were not to be sold ahead of schedule.

The low income from the administration of federal property was due to the fact that a considerable part of the dividends and income from leasing federal property seemed always to get diverted away from the budget proper and in other directions, such as joint-stock companies (Gazprom, EES Rossii, LUKoil and others), state bodies (Ministry of Defense Industry, Ministry of Transportation, Ministry of Education, Ministry of Culture), and public organizations, in accordance with the privileges granted.

The main responsibility for budget items at the end of 1996 lay with the administrations of the State Property Committee, the Ministry of the Economy, and the Ministry of Finance. To be fair, I should note that as early as the spring our Committee requested that the Government lower the target figures, but this request was ignored at the ratification of the budget.

And as early as November I proposed, along with the above request, that we immediately sell the block of shares of EES Rossii; this could bring about two trillion rubles into the budget before the end of the year. The tender for the search of a financial consultant to sell 7.5% of the company stock had already been awarded in August to a consortium of leading investment banks headed by Credit Suisse First Boston. The work on structuring the deal was well under way when we suddenly faced staunch resistance from the Fuel and Energy Ministry. The minister, Petr Rodionov, categorically denied the necessity of selling the shares of EES Rossii, arguing that such a sale would reduce the State's management control over it. His position was difficult to understand, as it contradicted two Presidential decrees that had explicitly ordered the sale of this stock. As for manageability, couldn't he comprehend that the 51% stake that would still be held by the State was enough to dispel such concerns?

THE PRIVATIZATION OF REAL ESTATE

Privatization of State and municipal enterprises peaked in 1992–94 and fell in 1996. But by then our focus had really shifted to real estate, including the land on which privatized assets were sitting. Large-scale privatization of land and the development of a real estate market were truly exciting developments, and they had become urgently required to increase the tax and rent income sent to the budget, in order for companies to utilize resources more effectively, and to improve the economy.

Sales of property being privatized were going up steadily. If in 1995 real estate sales constituted 16% of all privatization, ranking third after conversion of State enterprises into joint-stock companies and purchase of rented assets, during the first six months of 1996 this percentage went up to 22%, moving up to second place.

Privatization of land took the foreground in 1996. Obtaining the right to own land, a company received an opportunity to finance itself. As the most precious asset, land could be used as collateral for credit, expansion of production, renovation, or new construction. And the purchase of their land made enterprises considerably more attractive.

A deliberately excessive redemption price (200 times the land tax, fixed by a Government decree in November 1994) had previously made the purchase of the land underneath a company as good as impossible. This was perhaps the single worst roadblock still standing in the way of privatization. Thus it was with jubilation that we learned that a new normative price of land had been established by Presidential Decree No. 478 of May 11, 1995, namely, equal to 10 times the land tax. If we assume a threefold increase in general price levels during the inflationary period, the purchase price of the land still amounted to only 30 times the land tax. Now it finally became possible for a great many companies to purchase the land they up to now had only occupied.

All of a sudden companies realized that they could afford to buy the land they stood on at relatively low price, a vital step toward the creation of a single property unit that would include, as elsewhere in the world, both the land and the buildings and constructions located on it. The regions also received a tool for the management and control of real estate assets.

The purchase of land permitted the survival of enterprises having large production areas but declining production. Not only did the sale of surpluses become a way of improving a company's financial standing, but it was also the beginning of a real restructuring, redeployment, and revised methods of using industrial capacities, as operations were refined to focus on the main parcel of land.

CREATION OF THE REGISTER OF STATE PROPERTY ASSETS

By the end of 1996, the federal property register held data on 30,582 federal enterprises and organizations and 6,490 joint-stock companies, associations, and other enterprises of mixed forms of property whose stock had been assigned to federal property. A computerized entry was created for each piece of property, to be updated quarterly.

The job of keeping up the departmental registers of federal property was to be done by ministries and their departments. Thus the register's data could be displayed at regional, departmental, and branch levels; and it was integrated into the local computer network of our Committee, with access to all interested users.

In addition, it was at this point that we were able to feel greater confidence due to the completely rewritten new Civil Code adopted at this time in Russia, which brought about numerous changes in the field of property relations, security transactions, the scale of privatization, and the delimiting of property. Among other consequences, these changes in turn necessitated basic changes in the status of the register and its handling. The register definitely had to have extradepartmental status; and adding the data to its database had to be carried out in cooperation with the holders of principal State information resources—the Single State Register of Enterprises of the State Committee for Statistics, the State register of companies for the tax service, and the branch *kadastres*, tax registers for land, water, forests, and mineral deposits. Finding a solution to these questions required commissioning thorough studies at considerable expense.

Besides maintaining the register, there is another very important type of activity that adds to the security and smooth functioning of the financial system, i.e., depository activity, which can be carried out by legal entities that are professional traders at the equity market. The depository of the State Property Committee itself did not meet the Federal Commission for Securities (FKTsB)'s requirements; all it did was conserve the share certificates in State property. Since the Committee wasn't formally a professional trader at the equity market either, it couldn't carry out depository activity; but we upgraded the register to conform with the FKTsB's requirements, and duly presented all the necessary documents for its licensing.

In my opinion, it has become an urgent task to organize a tender for the right to be the State depository, empowered to keep all the State's certificates, so that the entire list of State property may be concentrated in one place.

DIVIDENDS ON SHARES IN FEDERAL OWNERSHIP
The income from the use of stock held in federal property is essentially the dividends from this stock. In 1996 only 120 billion rubles were received as dividends. Starting from the nominal value of the State portfolio of shares, amounting to 7 trillion rubles, the federal budget earned a 2% annual income on its shares, which was one-tenth of the inflation rate at that time—an unacceptable return for any conscientious proprietor. In view of the inflation forecast for 1997, we set the total amount of dividends on federal blocks of shares at 1.5 trillion rubles.

The verifications of the State Tax Service, together with territorial Committees for Property Management, showed that approximately half the companies reviewed did not pay dividends on their shares because they had no net profit from the year's results. Most of the companies that did post a profit decided not to pay dividends on ordinary shares, including those in State property. To be fair, I should note that the use of dividends for purposes not connected with filling the federal budget was stipulated by a whole range of documents. As for these joint-stock companies, we thought one of the most important tasks of the State representatives was verifying the purposeful use of these dividends. Exemptions from paying dividends into the federal budget had been introduced in 1992–93, when enterprises were becoming companies, but by 1996 it had became obvious that in most cases these exemptions had to be abrogated. The budget had to be bolstered through the ownership, use, and control of shares.

COMPARATIVE ANALYSIS OF THE PERFORMANCE OF STATE-OWNED AND PRIVATIZED COMPANIES

Privatization is admittedly only one method of managing State property. Too often the efficiency of this method was judged on the basis of an erroneous premise, namely that privatization must be an endless source of revenue for the budget. The practice of most countries with transitional economies points in the opposite direction. It is unrealistic to hope to receive large resources from the privatization of State enterprises that produce uncompetitive products with worn-out equipment. Privatization can guarantee revenue inflow into the budget *only by creating private companies that manufacture products that can generate high profits*, which can be taxed. All the experience we have gained in five years has shown us that attempts to attract investment while privatization is actually being carried out always end in failure. Rather, privatization creates a *mechanism for attracting investments*; whether investment will actually come depends on other factors, such as the inflation rate, political stability, and the bank rate.

At the same time, another public myth has emerged: that after privatization companies are worse off, or simply collapse, "looted by new managers." This is incendiary political thinking, and has had to be countered with facts. Thus, in the spring of 1996, the Duma commissioned experts in both St. Petersburg and Moscow to conduct a comparative analysis of the economic results of companies with different shareholding structures.

The commission analyzed trends in economic indicators for State and privatized enterprises during the period 1993–95. The data were broken down industry by industry, from the point of view of both sector and production scale and according to the point in time when the company in question began being privatized.

The actual sample consisted of 2,438 enterprises in eight industries (machine tools, ferrous and nonferrous metallurgy, chemicals, light industry, and the food, medical, and construction-materials industries). Results were compared according to three groups of companies: 575 State enterprises, 596 joint-stock companies with more than a 25% State-owned interest, and 1,267 joint-stock companies with less than a 25% State-owned interest.

The survey revealed that privatized companies considerably outperformed State enterprises in main economic indices. Moreover, the lower the share of the State in the enterprise was, the better its financial results.

Productivity is a greater factor in the discrepancy between privatized companies and State enterprises even when their financial indicators show less of a difference. This is explained by the fact that after privatization, companies become more enterprising, are ready to take greater risks, make more investments, and take out credits for those investments. This somewhat lowers their financial indicators while raising productivity, profitability, capital turnover—and, dare I say it, social utility.

The analysis of economic indicators for companies with different forms of property showed that in general, privatized companies in 1995—compared to 1994—showed the greatest increase in production and profit, and thus were the main factor in the normalization of the economic situation and the principal source of budgetary revenues. On the whole, the State sector suffered a decrease of 17%; companies at a medium level of privatization saw their production volume increase by 12.5%, and enterprises at a high level of privatization by 16.1%. The average listed number of employees in groups of privatized companies decreased in different periods and in different paces. The main decrease took place in 1994, by approximately 9% compared to 1993. Nevertheless, the surprising fact is that in 1995, compared to 1994, the number of employees actually *grew* by 13% in companies at a medium level of privatization and by almost 7% in enterprises at a high level of privatization. Simultaneously, State enterprises showed a steady, though small, decrease during these two periods, of 4% per year.

Finally, the comparative analysis of the groups of privatized enterprises, broken down according to the duration of the "private" period, showed the longer the period since the beginning of privatization, the higher the level of business activity of the enterprise, and the better its financial situation.

CHAPTER VI

THE HOT
SUMMER OF 1997

P rivatization in economic reform is really aimed at making the economy more efficient; it is just one of the many tools needed to achieve this objective. We cannot yet be fully content with the results achieved, even granted that they have definite significance—which may be more due to the poisonous backdrop of opposition to reforms and the inconsistency that characterized our methods at the time against which one sees these results, and gives them a triumphant quality.

True, the immediate objectives of privatization—the liquidation of the monopoly exercised by State property in the economy and the creation of both an equity market and a large social layer of private proprietors (shareholders)—have been indisputably achieved during the past five years.

In 1997, the capitalization of Russian companies experienced sudden and significant growth; we went through a new upsurge of market capitalization, as seen in the example of EES Rossii, a unified energy company in charge of all power stations in the country, which was sold in January for $370 million. (As of this writing, this organization is benefiting from the leadership of Anatoly Chubais, who took over as head after leaving the Government.)

More precisely, the period started with Boris Yeltsin's victory in June 1996; its nature stemmed from understanding that from now on companies were going to cost a lot more, and would not be as easy to sell. That is why shares in big blocks could only be put on the market very carefully and professionally; otherwise the market could crash. This was the big change from the beginning of privatization, when the market was ready to swallow up any volume of shares.

Nineteen ninety-seven was an eventful year for me; a few months after I had completed this manuscript and submitted it to the publishers, many things changed in my life.

In March, following a new reshuffling of the Cabinet of Ministers, I was appointed Deputy Prime Minister in the Russian Government. I wanted to oppose this appointment as I had no desire to rise that high in the Government, but Chubais, who had once again become the First Deputy Prime Minister, persuaded me to accept, promising I would be able to step down— after the annual target for privatization receipts had been met. (At the April session of Government, when the 1996 results of privatization were reviewed, he also casually got the target figures increased from 6.5 to 10 trillion rubles, and the GKI had to integrate this unofficial objective into its program. Our friendship was not affected.)

THE DUMA'S FAVORITE BETE NOIRE

In June 1996, the Duma reviewed the results of privatization yet again. This subject was as always the favorite bete noire of the leftist opposition, and now a special plenary session of the Duma was called. For some reason, to most Duma members every privatization project is evil incarnate. I am not questioning their sincerity, but I do insist that their positions are politically motivated.

Besides the Duma, the State Audit Office—and the General Prosecutor's Office taking cues from the State Audit Office—took an unusual amount of interest in the subject. This was probably because the activities of the State Property Committee, as compared to other departments, have always been more visible, effective, and politically substantive.

Now, the State Audit Office strikes me as an extremely partisan body. Among its decisions, I have yet to see *one* that favored privatization. If it had been truly nonpartisan, one would have expected to hear at least a few pluses and minuses cited on this issue. But that office was created only to verify budgetary flow, not to make political comments! One of its tasks is to determine whether there has been a violation of law or damage to the budget. Accordingly, it has to operate within a clear frame of reference, for there are some privatization projects clearly designed for the budget—something, by the way, that has never been recognized by the State Audit Office.

There was a difference of political opinion in the Duma, to put it mildly, in dealing with privatization matters. One group was dominated by the Communists, Liberal-Democrats, and Agrarians, all irreconcilable adversaries of privatization. The second, less numerous group consisting of the NDR (Russia Our Home) and Yabloko delegates, focused their complaints only on demands for the correction of abuses that they saw as having existed during privatization; and they went further to specify that the remedies they sought would be legislative or judicial, not political—they weren't interested in revenge against villains or shake-ups in administrations, just in laws improved and conflicts resolved.

One example of such an "abuse" may suffice: There had been instances of auctions of properties in remote regions being won by single bidders, because in many of the most remote regions there was obviously no other entity available with the capability, resources, and desire to be involved with the enterprise in question, so no one else could be found who would bid. The law required more than one bidder for a sale to go through, but in practice we allowed many of these single bidders to be successful. Thus their proprietorship of the shares they had bought and paid for remained vulnerable to court challenge, a fact with potentially undesirable if as yet undefined possible consequences. NDR and Yabloko delegates desired normalization of the settlement of such claims.

Although both radical and moderate members of the Duma Commission that analyzed the results of privatization in 1992–96 made plenty of critical remarks, maybe the latter managed to convince their orthodox colleagues that they had to stay within the limits of their constitutional powers, because the draft of the resolution was quite mild and used legally correct formulations.

At the Commission's request, a special investigation took place the day before the Duma hearings. The experts invited to testify used a representative sample to compare three types of companies: State enterprises, privatized companies with over 25% State ownership, and, finally, fully privatized companies.

Once more a study showed that the fully privatized enterprises performed better than the enterprises with a large State block of shares, and that the latter, in turn, performed better than the State enterprises. The experts also found that the difference in efficiency *grew each year after privatization.*

Thus, the study conducted by our opponents revealed that privatization had an undeniably healthy effect on our economy, and that without it the economic situation would have been far worse. (I personally don't see how it could have yielded different results.) Yet even this study failed to mollify the majority of deputies at the plenary session. They voted for a decree that reiterated their resentment of privatization and recommended that the Government turn to arbitration courts to review privatization decisions that, according to them, violated the law. Moreover, in one of the amendments introduced by the Communists, the General Prosecutor was once again advised to indict the officials "who organized and conducted unlawful privatization in the country." They also recommended that the President "decide whether the main agents of privatization were competent for the job." They meant Chubais and myself, of course.

I believe that there is a cardinal difference between revising the results of privatization and legally revoking any decisions that violated the law. I am categorically against the former and totally in favor of the latter. One welcomes revocation of illegal decisions, since it advances economic activity. That is why, in spite of everything, I was determined to fully cooperate with the Duma. Merely calling them "fools" belonged in the past. I thought we had agreed that State property had to be sold at a high price, and that we could move together in that direction. As a first step, I proposed that the Duma delegate representatives to the GKI board. We are not a closed order of monks, I said, but an open organization, and we did not harbor any grudges. The deputies showed no particular enthusiasm for my proposal.

I do not wish to pat myself on the back, but working with the Duma had some positive political results. Only a month after this discussion, the Duma ratified by a constitutional majority a new law on privatization of State and municipal enterprises, one that came to grips with new realities like complicated investment instruments and the finer mechanics and legalities of international financial cooperation.

THE TYUMEN OIL COMPANY

In July, the Tyumen Oil Company (TNK) scandal broke. We had planned to sell 40% of this company's stock with an investment auction, and the struggle for control of TNK heated up as soon as the auction date was announced. In this colorful affair we had a determined opponent, the managing director of the company, Viktor Paliy, who also ran the Nizhnevartovskneftegaz (NNG) Company. A classic holdover Soviet-era manager, he had treated and regarded himself as the owner for years, doing whatever he pleased and embezzling as much as he could. Needless to say, he was passionately opposed to the privatization of his company (and would soon be fired by the new owners, the Alfa Bank Group, by the way).

(Again, a note: the reader may remember me complaining about the broken promises that were generated by the early investment auctions; in this later period, we had worked out ways of being more sure that the promised investments would be forthcoming: typically, they were structured in the form of the settlement of outstanding debts to the Government itself, a commitment we did not have difficulty keeping track of! In any case, this was the last one we ever did.)

TNK was a leading oil extraction enterprise, located above the Arctic Circle. Paliy insisted that the auction be postponed or even canceled. In his opinion, the future privatization of TNK was contrary to State interests, and the terms and conditions of the auction were "written to favor" a specific investor—the Alfa group.

We made several attempts to remove Viktor Paliy from the leadership of NNG and from TNK's board of directors, but nothing worked. First Yury Shafranik, chairman of the TNK board of directors, arrived too late for the NNG shareholders' meeting, where he had planned to cast the State's vote against Paliy's reelection as mannaging director. Curiously, his plane could not land at the Nizhnevartovsk airport in perfectly clear weather. Second, at the TNK shareholders' meeting, Nikolai Rusanov, the State representative and head of the relevant department of the Fuel and Energy Ministry, filled in his voting slip incorrectly. So Paliy was elected to the board and the candidacy of Yury Shafranik was rejected, owing to this "mistake" (he was to become chairman of the board later).

Nikolai Rusanov wrote a sincerely contrite note, asking our indulgence over the fact that he had forgotten to put Shafranik's name on his ballot. I called the commission in charge of counting votes at the meeting and asked that the vote be corrected, considering the functionary's mistake. The TNK representatives refused to honor my request.

It was crazy—we owned more than 90% of the equity capital in the company and still could not appoint people to its management board or oppose those we did not want! The owner could not pursue his policy in the company because the people whom we had appointed were simply scared.

I thought of the books by Alexandre Dumas I had read as a child, in which he describes the "fun fights" between the Royal Musketeers and Cardinal's Guards. Well, our fights were anything but "fun."

Viktor Paliy launched a full-scale offensive. At one of his press conferences, he even publicly proclaimed an "enemies list." My name led the list, although when he read it out he added, "to my great regret." (I suppose he wanted me to feel that I had disappointed him.) It preceded the name of the head of the Federal Insolvencies Department (FUDN), Petr Mostovoy, who was about to start a liquidation procedure against Nizhnevartovskneftegaz, which had run up debts of some three million rubles to budgets of different levels, as well as those of Mikhail Fridman, the head of the Alfa group, and Yury Shafranik, the former (and future) chairman of the TNK board of directors.

Every weapon was employed: letters to government top executives, statements in which Duma deputies stated their support for Paliy, and numerous attacks in the media. Paliy's greatest "success" was a two-hour-long press conference before a packed audience on the subject of corruption and privatization.

Theatrically rolling his eyes and clenching his fists, Paliy spoke about the interests of the State being violated "by the so-called reformers and by people once called rootless cosmopolites" (in Russia a crystal-clear reference to Jews). He called the privatization of TNK nothing more than "a State act of piracy against a State company." Watching him, my conviction that he would have made a great actor was confirmed.

Paliy's furious warfare did yield some fruit. A specially formed commission of the Fuel and Energy Ministry conducted an inquiry on the terms of the auction and issued a recommendation that "any inequality between participants" must be avoided. General Prosecutor of the Russian Federation Yury Skuratov sent a letter to the President requesting the cancellation of the TNK investment auction.

Perhaps Skuratov did not know that a day earlier, President Yeltsin had appointed Boris Nemtsov and myself to supervise the auction personally and ordered as well the "observance of all its terms and conditions" (which, I might add, were not specified in the President's order).

Paliy's histrionics were totally divorced from reality. In blaming us for trying to sell TNK, "the pearl of Samotlor," at a bargain price, he somehow forgot that a few months earlier he had asked the Government to give him the 91% of TNK stock that was in federal property into a trusteeship for a three-year period.

I myself was convinced that TNK needed to be sold earlier, so that the new head of the company could grasp all the problems it was facing, but the auction took place on July 18, as scheduled. The arbitration court of the Tyumen region had ruled a postponement just a few days earlier, but revoked its resolution hours before the deadline for submitting bids. The successful bidder (a total of five candidates took part in the contest) was the New Holding Company, which paid over $800 million for a 40% block of shares (investments included), while the terms of the auction stipulated an actual payment of only about $160 million.

I would rather not dwell on the subsequent fate of TNK and Viktor Paliy, the Oil Tycoon of Nizhnevartovsk. His relations with the new senior management of TNK would make a separate story, no less gripping.

SVYAZINVEST 1997

We had by now analyzed in depth our failure with Svyazinvest in 1995 and had drawn a number of conclusions. There had been subjective reasons: there hadn't been enough time to carry out the operation (we hadn't started until August, although we wanted to complete it in December). But there were also objective reasons, justly presented to us by the potential buyer, the Italian company STET.

The main reason, I think, was that the telecommunications sector at that time was badly structured. All local operators were joined into the Svyazinvest holding company, and all interurban and international communications were in Rostelekom, which was independent of Svyazinvest. In this way, though the two companies were officially in the same market, they did not compete, since they worked in different market segments. In effect, we had two monopolies for the two kinds of telecommunications. This situation had all the flaws inherent in a monopoly without its merits, like a clear and well-defined relationship between the subdivisions. Besides, this reduced the capitalization of Svyazinvest in its existing form. How was it possible to acquire shares of Svyazinvest if no clear and understandable relations with Rostelekom existed? It was hard to understand how Svyazinvest could break into the interurban and international communications market.

We faced hard choices: Without optimal structuring of the sector, we could not decide on an efficient method of privatization. We turned to our consultants from the World Bank and to the NM Rothschild & Sons investment bank. They proposed several ways to structure the sector: a full partnership with Rostelekom, creating six or seven subregional companies entitled to issue services on the interurban and international markets, or the privatization of Svyazinvest separately from Rostelekom under a cartel agreement. There were a few other, lesser options. In terms of capitalization of the sector, the second scenario seemed the most expedient, although it was almost impractical in organizational terms. We therefore opted for a full merger, i.e., the injection of the controlling stake of Rostelekom into the charter capital of Svyazinvest.

We understood that a full monopolization of the sector ran counter to sacred free-market principles. However, we also knew of countries with fully formed market economies where effective State control allows telecommunication monopolies to operate with a fair degree of efficiency. Our choice was based on the prag-matic need to attract major resources from privatization, since we had already predicted an acute budgetary crisis, a perennial phe-nomenon in Russia (this may already have occurred to you).

We began the implementation of our plan at the end of 1996. There were tough negotiations with lawyers on the wording of a Presidential decree to create a new structure for the sector. Pre-paring the decree took almost six months, until about May 1997. At the same time we began an active search for potential par-ticipants in the tender for the sale of 25% of stock in the new Svyazinvest, which would include Rostelekom. For the first time in the history of Russian privatization, we drafted a circular let-ter (in Russian and English) and conducted a kind of road show in London and New York. We tried to make this operation as accessible as possible to potential investors.

Despite the hype, in the end only two consortia took part in the tender, which was held on July 25. One of them, TELEFAM BV, was created by the Alfa Bank together with MOST Bank; the other, MUSTCOM Ltd, by UNEXIM Bank together with Renais-sance-Kapital/Renaissance International Ltd. Both of these in-cluded Western investment groups like Credit Suisse First Boston and George Soros's Quantum Group, while Alfa's consortium also included a strategic investor, Telefonica de Espana SA, a Spanish telecommunications company.

We set the opening price at $1.2 billion, expecting to get $1.4–$1.5 billion at the most. The competition between the two consortia was so intense it drove the price to $1.875 billion. MUSTCOM won the auction. Yet there was a downside to it, too, as (typically) a normal Russian business competition turned into a political conflict. Predictably, the loser blames the organizers of the tender rather than himself, and imputes to them some fantastic motivations.

The day before the auction, at an extended Government session, Chernomyrdin saw it coming, and turning to me suddenly, said, "It is too early to get relaxed, Kokh. Every time you have a collateral or investment auction, there is a scandal, and with serious fallout!"

It was as if he had been looking into a crystal ball. The scandal—an "information war," the media called it—began the next day and has not abated since. I warned that this would happen at a press conference held right after the auction to announce the results. I was certain there would be an orchestrated media campaign against this deal. However, in my opinion this is the best evidence that the deal was a success.

We were accused of selling the stock of the largest telecommunications company too cheaply, particularly in comparison to such countries as Hungary, Romania, and the Czech Republic. Nobody seemed to remember that in those Eastern European countries, the majority blocks of shares sold belonged to companies that were communication operators. We, by contrast, sold a financial holding, which had no operating license from the Russian Ministry of Communications. Moreover, we sold a blocking, not a controlling, amount of shares, which is why our expectations had been modest.

We were accused of backroom dealing; the pledge auctions were held openly, in front of cameras, yet this did not protect us from the accusations of being closed, and today the pledge auctions are considered the model of favoritism. This is why we kept the Svyazinvest deal maximally open to investors and relatively open to the media.

One of the most important results of the auction was that this time capital came to Russia, rather than Russian securities being exported abroad. I think that the 1997 deal turned out to be 4.5 times as effective as the failed sale of the same block of shares to the Italian company STET in 1995. The conditions of that deal provided that the greatest part of the money would go for investment in the company, with only $400 million going to the budget. But the transaction did not take place, and even this sum did not go to the budget, so I consider all the comparisons irrelevant.

At long last we had established a new pattern of selling high where the deal is prepared carefully and without undue haste. I hope this pattern will continue in the future.

NORILSKY NICKEL

Ten days after the Svyazinvest auction, the stake in Norilsky Nickel, pledged in 1995, was put up for sale. This was preceded by intrigue worthy of a Hollywood thriller. The hostilities broke out when the potential buyer, the Trans World Group we knew very well, did not like the declared terms of the auction. The company representatives said they were ready to invest up to a billion dollars for the block of shares offered for sale.

213

A few days before the results were announced (a standard practice used to minimize the response time), Chernomyrdin received a letter from General Prosecutor Yury Skuratov, in which the latter asked to stop the securities auction. The auction commissioner (UNEXIM) was the entity selling the stock and should have been addressed. (This was one of those cases where a bank was acting as broker for the State and keeping 30% of the profit. The pledge period had expired, and Skuratov knew that the Government, having failed to pay back the loan, had to yield ownership and control to the bank, and that it was the bank that had control now, but sent the letter improperly to Chernomyrdin anyway, who initially went along with it, even though it was illegal. Skuratov soon withdrew the letter.)

Skuratov was breaking the law writing at the last minute to the Prime Minister to try to get him involved. Failing to understand the situation, Chernomyrdin ordered the auction stopped, in contravention of the Civil Code. By law, after the expiration date the auction organizer has the right to dispose of deposited blocks of shares at his discretion, including the right to sell them by any means provided by the law.

I was in a bind. On the one hand, I had a direct order from my direct superior, the Prime Minister, to stop the auction; on the other hand, how could I do this if I had not violated the law?

Had a similar event occurred a year earlier, the fate of the operation would have been sealed. No one would have dared disobey the head of the Government. But we felt we were on sound legal ground, and so we decided to fight.

At first, on the day of the auction, I instructed the State representatives in the commission (specifically, my deputy Sergey Molozhavy) to vote for postponement. This way, I was officially executing the Prime Minister's order. Then I went to the General

Prosecutor's office. By midday, Deputy General Prosecutor Yury Chaika and I had sent the Prime Minister a joint letter in which we pointed out that there were no legal grounds for stopping the auction: "...the vendor of the block of shares is the commissioner itself ('MFK Moscow Partners'). The decision to stop the auction therefore lies solely with the MFK Moscow Partners and is outside the jurisdiction of GKI and RFFI." We indicated that, since the legal impact of the auction would be felt only after the results were announced, it was necessary to examine whether its terms and results comply with the existing legislation without bringing the auction to a halt. We explained that the only option for discontented parties was to dispute the results of the auction in court after they had been published.

The Prime Minister took a decision worthy of Solomon: he ordered that it be examined "whether the auction's results comply with existing legislation, regardless of the results." On the one hand, he agreed that the government must not violate the Civil Code and its resolutions. On the other hand, however, he stated that the agreement with the auction winner could be terminated only *after* the conclusions on the failure of the terms and results of the auction to comply with existing laws had been reached and announced.

Once again, despite the many obstacles, the auction took place. It was won by the Swift Company, which bid $680 million, with an opening price of some $570 million. The winner was acting on behalf of the UNEXIM group. Consequently, the State not only paid off the credits it had previously obtained with the shares in Norilsky Nickel as collateral, but also received an inflow of some half a trillion rubles into the budget. The investigation into the legality and terms of the auction only confirmed our belief that no violations could be proven.

After the Norilsky Nickel sale, I clearly realized that no auction could take place without screaming and hysteria. In any auction, there is a winner and there is a loser. And I guess there are a few reasons, ranging from the lack of a civilized business tradition to a lack of general culture, why the loser here in Russia grabs every opportunity to wring his hands in public.

Yet for me the sales of Svyazinvest and Norilsky Nickel, which by the end of the summer had brought some 10 trillion rubles into the State budget instead of the planned 6.4 trillion, were the last straw. Usually I accepted personal attacks with total calm, but a critical mass seemed to have been reached, and I decided that the time had come to leave State service. The day before going on vacation I sent Chubais a letter tendering my resignation. A few days later, on August 13, while I was visiting the United States, I received news that President Yeltsin had accepted my resignation.

I trust that my colleagues and friends in the Government do not bear me a grudge. Once the task entrusted to me was completed, I left office with a clear conscience, having proven that privatization could contribute billions of dollars to the budget. In no way do I regret my work in the Government; I learned a lot under the leadership of Prime Minister Chernomyrdin, and I am grateful to him for the constant support he extended to me. He publicly announced that he was bewildered by my departure: I must be the first Deputy Prime Minister who resigned of his own accord.

CONCLUSION

Today, we are in the autumn of 1997 and, fully reaping the fruits of that successful summer, I can honestly say that no law was violated at the Svyazinvest auction. We achieved what we had set out to do. We got the highest price then possible for the block of shares of the biggest telecommunications company. Nobody can convince me of the contrary.

I have a clear opinion on the value of this or that item: I am convinced that an item is worth exactly what people are prepared to pay for it at a given point in time. Many factors come into play: market capitalization, political risks, the company's assets and liabilities. In 1997, with political stability no longer a problem, confidence in the Russian market has increased greatly, which has caused an increase in the assets and capitalization of Russian companies. The sale of the controlling block of shares of

Svyazinvest confirmed this. As an example, I can say that during the privatization of telecom companies in Argentina and Chile, capitalization reached $400–$500 per telephone line, but that during the privatization of Svyazinvest capitalization reached $880 per telephone line—double the amount for those countries economically comparable to Russia.

However, this isn't the most important result of the auction, which became, through no fault of our own, the biggest scandal in the history of Russian privatization. It is no secret that the Russian state used to be largely dependent on capital. It was owning everything that made the State so monolithically powerful. Now that questions of power here, at long last, are more and more thoroughly a matter of the consent of the governed, the State is beginning to be weaned of this dependency, and is making every effort in this direction.

If the same rules used for the first time at the Svyazinvest auction are preserved in the future, the State authorities will gradually manage to wean themselves of their dependency on capital to the extent possible in a market economy. It is absolutely obvious that capital influences the state power like any other factor. The fact that at a certain stage the State fell into this dependency was economically conditioned. To build a market economy, the State, especially in a poor country like Russia, must look for a social base of support. In Russia, this base was the entrepreneurs. The State was supported by them and to some extent positively influenced by them. As the Government has proceeded to expand its support base and declared common playing rules, State power has become more and more independent of capital.

Perhaps a few years from now someone will elucidate the vicissitudes we experienced both during this period and in the aftermath of the Svyazinvest auction. But today, as the wounds still fester and animosity has not abated, I do not wish to dwell on this; the reader is free to peruse numerous publications, including the Western press, to appreciate the bitterness and tension that accompanied this event. Henceforth I see Russian privatization divided into two periods: the one before Svyazinvest and the one after it. The events that followed make a long, interesting, and quite different story.

TABLES

TABLE 1. SALE OF SHARES AT ALL-RUSSIAN
AND INTERREGIONAL SPECIALIZED AUCTIONS IN 1995

	BIDS RECEIVED		AMOUNTS PAID	
	Units	%	In Thousands of Rubles	%
Legal entities	298	10.9	654,782,170	84.1
Private individuals	2,432	89.1	124,230,070	15.9
Nonresidents	46	1.5	220,339,410	23

TABLE 2. RECEIPTS ALLOCATED TO THE FEDERAL BUDGET IN 1995
(IN BILLIONS OF RUBLES) FROM THE SALE AND THE
UTILIZATION OF STATE-OWNED PROPERTY.

Kind of revenue	According to plan (as stipulated in the Act of State Budget)	Transferred to the Federal Budget	Execution of the plan (%)
Receipts from the sale of state and municipal property	4,785.4	1,140.7	23.8%
Dividends on state-owned shareholdings	82.6	92.822	112.3%
Leasing of state property	123.8	116.714	94.2%
Settlement of debts to the State Budget of joint-stock companies whose stock has been pledged and sold through investment competitions	0	1,543.5	
Shares pledged	0	3,573.76	
NK "Lukoil" bonds	0	1000	
TOTAL	4,991.8	7,467.5	149.59%

**TABLE 3. EVOLUTION OF PRIVATIZATION
OF ENTERPRISES DURING THE PERIOD 1992-95**

Years	Number of privatized enterprises	Value of privatized property (millions rubles)	Sale price of enterprises (millions rubles)	Number of privatized enterprises as a percentage of total number of enterprises
1991-1992	48,295	20,799	164,678	19.2
1993	40,519	631,763	595,415	36.3
1994	23,811	439,193	851,499	47.0
1995	6,172	526,262	893,403	56.7
TOTAL	118,797	1,618,017	2,504,995	56.7

**TABLE 4. DISTRIBUTION OF PRIVATIZED
ENTERPRISES BY FORM OF OWNERSHIP AT THE END OF 1995**

Years	1991-1995	1995
Federal property	27,461	240
State property belonging to the subjects of the Russian Federation	14,862	788
Municipal property	76,474	5,144
TOTAL	118,797	6,172

**TABLE 5. DISTRIBUTION OF PRIVATIZED ENTERPRISES
BY FORM OF OWNERSHIP.**

Years	1993	1994	1995	1996
Municipal property	26,340	11,108	6,960	3,354
State property belonging to the subjects of the Russian Federation	9,521	5,112	1,317	715
Federal property	7,063	5,685	1,875	928
Total number of privatized enterprises	42,924	21,905	10,152	4,997

**TABLE 6. DISTRIBUTION OF PRIVATIZED ENTERPRISES
BY METHODS OF PRIVATIZATION DURING THE PERIOD 1993-96 (%).**

Years	1993	1994	1995	1996
Conversion of state enterprises into joint-stock	31.1	44.8	27.7	22.4
Sale at auctions	6.3	4.4	4.2	3.8
Commercial tenders	30.4	24.0	15.9	8.9
Investment contests	1.3	1.2	1.1	0.7
Redemption of leased property	29.5	20.8	29.8	32.0
Sale of property belonging to entities undergoing liquidation, already liquidated and uncompleted construction projects	0.4	1.5	4.2	5.7
Sale of real estate	-	-	15.4	22.9
Sale of land	-	-	0.6	1.5
Others	1.0	3.3	1.1	1.1
TOTAL	100.0	100.0	100.0	100.0

TABLE 7. MAIN CHARACTERISTICS OF JOINT-STOCK COMPANIES.

Years	1993	1994	1995	1996
Total number of joint-stock companies formed during the respective year	13,547	9,814	2,816	1,123
- including those characterized by the following forms of owner-ship at the time of privatization				
Municipal property	2,100	1,149	631	192
State property belonging to the subjects of the Russian Federation	6,028	3,744	859	393
Federal property	5,419	4,921	1,326	538
Registered share capital (billions rubles)	503	755	585	525.5
Join-stock companies whose controlling interests are assigned to the state or municipal property	439	1,496	698	190
- including those for which the ratio of assigned controlling block to registered share capital was:				
up to 15%	-	553 (36.9%)	48 (6.8%)	9 (4.7%)
16%-25%	-	158 (10.6%)	223 (31.9%)	63 (33.2%)
26%-38%	-	418 (27.9%)	189 (27.1%)	68 (35.8%)
39%-51%	-	278 (18.7%)	196 (28.1%)	40 (21%)
over 51%	-	89 (5.9%)	42 (6.1%	10 (5.3%)
Joint-stock companies with a golden share	204	792	429	132
Number of actions issued during the incorporation of joint-stock companies (in millions units)	695	1129	856	429.7

TABLE 8. SALE OF STOCK OF PRIVATIZED ENTERPRISES: PERFORMANCES OF THE RUSSIAN FEDERAL PROPERTY FUND IN 1996.

Method of sale	Nominal stock value (in billions rubles)	Receipts (in billions rubles)	Excess/nominal value ratio
Cash auction	0.2	7.41	37.1
Specialized auction	2.295	368.78	160.7
Investment contest	7.405	257.95	34.8
Commercial contest	0.83	48.79	58.8
Closed subscription	0.577	2.02	3.5
Enterprise Employees' Corporatization Fund (FARP)	5.127	26.93	5.3
TOTAL	16.434	711.88	43.3

PERSONALITIES

Mikhail BARSUKOV
> Head of Government Security, thereafter Head of the FSB, the successor of the KGB.

Sergey BELYAEV
> B. 1954, Ph.D. in Technical Sciences. Until September 1997 Chairman of the Duma's caucus of the political movement "Russia Our Home," headed by Chernomyrdin, then Premier.

Pavel BORODIN
> Manager of the President's households (cars, homes, dachas, etc.).

Yury CHAIKA
> First Deputy of the Prosecutor General of the Russian Federation.

Viktor CHERNOMYRDIN

B. 1938, Ph.D. in Technical Sciences. Premier of the Russian Federation December 1992–April 1998, 1985–89 Minister of Oil and Gas.

Anatoly CHUBAIS

B. 1955, Ph.D. in Economics. Head of the State's Energy Complex May 1998, 1991–94 Chairman of the State Committee for the Management of State Property, Nov. 1994–Jan. 1996 First Deputy Prime Minister, July 1996–March 1997 Head of the Executive Office of the President (Chief of Staff).

Anatoly FILATOV

Director of Norilsky Nickel.

Mikhail FRIEDMAN

B. 1964, Chairman of the Board of Directors of the Alfa Consortium.

Yegor GAIDAR

B. 1956, Ph.D. in Economics, leader of economic reforms under Yeltsin.

Viktor GERASHCHENKO

B. 1937, Expert in Finance, Chairman of the Central Bank, 1992–94. Since March 1994 CEO of the International Moscow Bank (MMB).

Sergey GLAZYEV

Ph.D. in Economics, Minister of Foreign Economic Relations, Member of the Duma.

Alexander HERZEN (1812–70)

Russian literary and political figure, founder of "Russian Socialism". In London he was founder and publisher of the almanac *Pole Star* (1855–68) and the newspaper *The Bell* (1857–67), leader of the political movement opposed to tsarism and serfdom.

Alexandr KAZAKOV

B. 1948, Ph.D. in Economics. January–June 1996 Deputy Prime Minister, Chairman of the State's Committee, from July 1996 First Deputy Director of the President's Staff (similar to the White House Chief of Staff).

Yury KOLPAKOV

Director of the Krasnoyarsk Aluminum Factory.

Anatoly KORABELSHCHIKOV

B. 1945, Engineer, Assistant to the President for Communications with the Regional Authorities.

Alexandr KORZHAKOV

Head of the President's Security Unit.

Valentin KOVALYOV

Former Minister of Justice.

Wassily LEONTIEFF

World-renowned economist, USA.

Oleg LOBOV

B. 1937, Ph.D. in Technical Sciences. Sept. 1993–June 1966 Head of the Security Council of the Russian Federation, June 1996–March 1997 First Deputy Prime Minister.

Vitaly MALKIN

B. 1952, President of the Rossiysky Kredit Bank.

Sergey MOLOZHAVY

B. 1961, Ph.D. in Technical Sciences. From Jan. 1997 State Secretary and Deputy Chairman of the State's Committee for the Management of State Property.

Petr MOSTOVOY

B. 1949. From 1995 Head of the Federal Agency in Charge of Bankruptcy.

Vitaly NAISHUL

President of the Institute of the National Economy, Introduced the idea of issuing vouchers in the early '80s.

Lyudmila NARUSSOVA

Wife of Anatoly Sobchak.

Viktor PALIY

Director of the Nizhnevartovsk Factory.

Vladimir POLEVANOV

Chairman of the State Committee for the Management of State Property, succeeding Chubais and followed by Belyaev.

Vladimir POTANIN

B. 1961. President of the UNEXIM Bank from 1993, from August 1996–March 1997 First Deputy Prime Minister, Expert in international relations.

Petr RODIONOV

B. 1951. Minister of Energy and Fuel, August 1996–April 1997.

Nikolai RUSANOV

Official at the Ministry of Energy and Fuel.

Yury SHAFRANIK

B. 1952. Former Head of the Tyumen Region, Jan. 1993–August 1996 Minister of Fuel and Energy, from April 1997 head of an energy company.

Alexandr SHOKHIN

B. 1951, Ph.D. in Economics. Head of the Duma caucus of the political movement "Russia Our Home."

Vladimir SHUMEIKO

First Deputy Prime Minister.

Yury SKURATOV

Prosecutor General of the Russian Federation.

Anatoly SOBCHAK

B. 1937, Ph.D. in Jurisprudence. Left Communist Party in 1990, Mayor of St. Petersburg June 1991–June 1996.

Oleg SOSKOVETS

First Deputy Prime Minister.

Vladimir YAKOVLEV

Governor of St. Petersburg.

Mikhail ZADORNOV

B. 1963, Ph.D. in Economics. Head of the Duma's committees on budget, taxation, banks, and finance and a member of the "Yabloko" movement headed by Grigory Yavlinsky. One of the coauthors of the famous plan "The 500 Days."

Valery ZUBOV

B. 1953, Ph.D. in Economics. 1993 elected to a five-year term as Governor of the Krasnoyarsk Region.

Gennady ZYUGANOV

B. 1944, Ph.D. in Social Sciences from the Communist Party Academy of Social Sciences. Head of the Communist caucus of Duma, 1996 Yeltsin's opponent for the Presidency.

AUTHOR'S BIOGRAPHY

Alfred R. Kokh was born on February 28, 1961, in the city of Zyryanovsk of the East Kazakhstan region. His father ran a transport garage in that city.

After graduating from High School No. 28 in 1978, he entered the Leningrad Institute of Finance and Economy. He graduated with a degree in mathematical economy and in 1983 entered graduate school at the same Institute. He received his Ph.D. degree in economics in 1987.

From 1987 to 1990, he worked as a junior research associate at the Prometheus Central Research Institute, then as a research assistant at the Department of Economy and Radio Electronic Production Management of the Leningrad Polytechnic Institute.

He entered the State Administration in 1990, when he became the Chairman of the Executive Committee of the Soviet People's Deputies of the Sestroretsk District (Leningrad region).

From 1991 on, Kokh's work was closely related to privatization and management of State property. In 1991–92 he was First Deputy Manager of the Leningrad State Property Fund. In 1992–93 he was the Deputy Chairman of the Committee for Managing St. Petersburg City Property.

On August 30, 1993, he was appointed Deputy Chairman of the Russian Federation State Committee for the Management of State Property. He was responsible for privatization in industry, in construction, in agroindustrial and defense sectors. In December 1994 he was officially honored by President of the Russian Federation Boris Yeltsin for the results of voucher privatization.

In March 1995, he was made First Deputy Chairman of the State Property Committee. He was responsible for the privatization of fuel and energy complexes, credit and finance sectors, and extractive industries. From August to September 1995, he was Acting Chairman of the Committee. In this capacity, he was one of the direct organizers of pledge auctions, which allowed the state to meet the budget target fixed for privatization revenues in 1995.

On September 12, 1996, he was appointed Chairman of the Russian Federation's State Committee for the Management of State Property.

. On March 17, 1997, by a Decree of the President, he was appointed Deputy Premier of the Russian Federation Government and Chairman of the Russian Federation State Committee for the Management of State Property.

On the August 13, 1997, he resigned both offices, at his own request.

Alfred Kokh is now Chairman of the Board of Montes Auri, an international investment company. He is married and lives with his wife and two daughters, aged 5 and 17 years old, in Moscow.

INDEX

A

Achinsk 73
Achinsk Alumina Complex 72, 74
Alfa Bank 114, 123–125, 206–208,
    211, 212
Alfa Laval 61
American deposit receipts 154
Arab countries 63
Arctic Circle 52
Argentina 63, 218
Arkhangelsk 59
Arkhangelsky Morskoy Torgovy Port
    110

B

Babayevskoye 123
Barsukov, Mikhail 34, 228
Belyaev, Sergey 31–33, 87, 89, 90,
    107, 156, 228
Berezovsky, Boris 12, 15, 16, 21
Bioprotsess 62
Bor 110

Borodin, Pavel 160, 228
Bratsk 74
Brazil 63, 167
British Gas 30

C

Cash Department 157
Central Bank 73, 98, 112, 123, 124,
    174, 185
Chaika, Yury 215, 228
Chechen war 68
Chernomyrdin, Viktor 11, 77, 78, 90,
    116, 125, 158, 161, 192, 212,
    214, 216, 229
Chile 218
China 63
Chita 59
Chubais, Anatoly 19, 20, 26–28, 31,
    32, 34, 36, 38, 73, 74, 76, 107,
    131, 134, 156, 159, 202, 205,
    216, 229
Committee for Budget 152

Committee for State Property Management 32, 50, 92, 190
Counterintelligence Division for Industrial Espion 70
Credit Suisse First Boston 211
Czech Republic 57, 212

D

Department for Supervision of Territorial Property 157
Dresdner Kleinwort Benson 12
Duma 17, 23, 25, 26, 72, 94, 99, 100, 105, 114, 128, 129, 134, 150–153, 156–160, 177, 184, 199, 203–206, 208
Dumas, Alexandre 208

E

Eastern Europe 57, 212
Eastern Oil Company
    See: Vostochnaya Oil Company
EES
    See: Unified Energy Systems of Russia
Employees Incorporation Fund 143, 190

F

FARP
    See: Employees Incorporation Fund
Federal Insolvencies Department 87, 208
Federal Nationalization Law 74
Federal Securities Committee 138
Federal Security Service 69
Federal Stock Corporation 139, 140
Filatov, Anatoly 158, 229
Financial-industrial groups 168
Foreign investment 29, 40, 54, 59, 60, 62, 63, 66, 67, 75, 110, 111, 137, 155, 187, 188
France 163, 167
Fridman, Mikhail 208, 229

FPGs
    See: Financial-industrial groups
FUDN
    See: Federal Insolvency Department

G

Gaidar, Yegor 25 36, 73, 134, 229
Gazprom 16, 38, 44, 53, 179, 180, 193
GDP
    See: Gross domestic product
General Prosecutor's Office 159,169, 203, 214
George Soros's Quantum Group 212
Gerashchenko, Viktor 73, 229
Germany 39, 59, 61, 62, 144
GKI
    See: State Property Committee
GKO
    See: Government short-term bond
Glazyev, Sergey 151, 229
Gorbachev, Mikhail 24, 48, 50
Government short-term bond 94, 95, 112, 192
Great Britain 30, 61, 162
Gross domestic product 39, 57
Gusinsky, Vladimir 12, 21

H

Henkel 144
Herzen, Alexander 163, 229
Hungary 212

I

Ignatiyev, Sergey 28
IMF
    See: International Monetary Fund
India 167
Inkombank 114, 126, 127
International Monetary Fund 91, 150–153
Investment funds 138

Irkutsk 74
Italy 163, 167

J

Japan 62

K

Kaliningrad 61
Kazakhstan 160
Kazakov, Alexandr 157–159, 161, 230
KGB 34, 69
Khodorkovsky, Mikhail 12
Kiriyenko, Sergey 11, 20, 36
Kirovlesprom 110
Kolpakov, Yury 69–71, 230
Komi Republic 59
KomiTEK 140–142
Korabelshchikov, Anatoly 115, 230
Korzhakov, Alexandr 34, 230
Kostroma 77
Kovalev, Valentin 124, 230
Krasnodar 140
Krasnoyarsk 68–70, 72, 74, 79, 115, 116
Krasnoyarsk Aluminum Plant 67
Krasnoyarsk Aluminum Stock Company 72
Krasnoyarsk Non-Ferrous 116
Kraz 68, 69, 72
KUGI
    See: Committee for State Property Management
Kulikov, Anatoly 18, 20

L

LAGUNA 123
Lebedinsky 55
Lenin 35, 36
Leontieff International Center for Social and Economic Research 32, 146
Leontieff, Wassily 32, 230
Liberal-Democratic party 134
Lobov, Oleg 77, 230

LOMO (Leningrad Optical and Mechanical Association 61
LUKoil 44, 89, 101, 110, 119, 131, 132, 145, 154, 179, 191, 193

M

Malkin, Vitaly 121, 230
Mardima 61
MENATEP 15, 104, 123–126
MENATEP/YUKOS 12
Mexico 63, 66, 68, 167
Mikrodin 62
Molozhavy, Sergey 214, 230
Moscow 31, 32, 36, 57, 59, 61, 71, 78, 122, 125, 127, 140, 190, 207
Moscow Currency Exchange 56
Mosenergo 154
MOST Bank 15, 211
Mostovoy, Petr 159, 161, 230
Murmanskoye Morskoye Parokhodstvo 110
MUSTCOM 211, 212

N

Naishul, Vitaly 25–27, 230
Narussova, Lyudmila 33, 231
NDR
    See: Russia Our Home, party
Nemtsov, Boris 19, 36, 209
Nizhnevartovsk 207
Nizhnevartovskneftegaz 206–208
Nizhny Novgorod 140
NNG
    See: Nizhnevartovskneftegaz
Nominal Privatization Act 26
Norilsky Nickel 13, 52, 53, 110, 114–116, 118–120, 122, 127, 155, 158, 159, 213, 215, 216
NORSIoil 179
Novolipetsk Metallurgy Complex 61
Novorossiyskoye Morskoye Parokhodstvo 110
Novosibirsk Electrode Plant 179
Noyabrneftegaz 126
NTV, TV channel 21, 22

O

Oil Finance Company 126
Oil Financing Company (NFK) 13
Omsk Refinery 126
ONAKO 153, 179
Opposition 129, 134, 143, 201
   –communist opposition 46, 74
   –leftist opposition 203
   –opposition to privatization 81
   –political opposition 46
ORT, TV channel 16, 21, 22

P

Paliy, Viktor 206–209, 231
Parliament
   See: Duma
PIFs
   See: Investment funds
Pikalevsk Alumina complex 74
Polevanov, Vladimir 68, 74–78, 81,
   87, 151, 231
Potanin, Vladimir 100, 103, 231
Potok stock company 61
President's Control Department 156
Private sector 26, 39, 42, 47, 50, 53,
   161, 163, 166, 190
Prosecutor General's Office 160
Public Prosecutor's Office 156
Public Prosecutor's regional office 72

R

Renaissance-Kapital/Renaissance In-
   ternational 211
RFFI
   See: Russian Fund for Federal
   Property
Rockefellers 40
Rodionov, Petr 193, 231
Romania 212
Rosgosstrakh 154
Rosneft 12, 154, 179, 180
Rosprom-YUKOS 14
Ross-gosstrakh 179
Rossiysky Kredit 114, 120–125

Rostelekom 54, 61, 112, 140, 210,
   211
Rusanov, Nikolai 207, 231
Russia Our Home, party 89, 134,
   203, 204
Russia Our Life 90
Russian Fund for Federal Property
   72, 92, 101, 102, 108, 122, 125,
   139, 142, 159, 160, 168, 190,
   191, 215
Russian securities market 95
Russian Trading System (RTS) 56
Russian Unified Energy Systems
   101, 140, 141, 154, 179, 193,
   202
Russky Kapital 68, 72
Rybkin, Ivan 90

S

Salamander 61
SAMEKO 126
SBS-Agro 12
Schwing-Stetter 61
Securities and Exchange Commis-
   sion in the U.S. 28
Shafranik, Yury 207, 208, 231
Shokhin, Alexandr 73, 231
Shumeiko, Vladimir 128, 231
Siberia 52, 69, 74, 126, 138
Sibneft 13, 15, 110, 114, 126, 141,
   179, 180, 191
SIBUR 153
SIDANKO 110, 114, 141, 154, 179
Skuratov, Yury 3, 125, 209, 214,
   231
Sobchak, Anatoly 31–34, 231
Soros, George 44, 45, 59
Soskovets, Oleg 34, 158
St. Petersburg 25, 28, 31–35, 57, 61,
   90, 116, 160, 173, 219
St. Petersburg Committee for State
   Property Manage 31
St. Petersburg Seaport 179
State Audit Office 156, 158–161,
   203

State Committee for Anti-Trust Policy 169
State Committee for Privatization 26
State Committee for Statistics 50
State Committee for the Management of State Property 71
State Property Committee 31, 68, 73, 75, 76, 78, 87, 89, 92, 96, 98, 106–108, 115, 122, 124, 125, 127–130, 134, 136, 140, 142, 144, 152, 153, 155–162, 164, 165, 168–170, 174, 175, 179, 186, 190, 191, 193, 196, 202, 203, 205, 215
State Property Fund 36, 37
Steimatz, Benjamin 59
STET, Italian company 133–135, 210, 213
Stolichny Savings Bank 126
Stumhammer 61
Sverdlovsk 115
Svyazinvest 13–15, 19, 54, 89, 101, 133, 134, 145, 153, 177, 179, 182, 184, 210, 211, 213, 216–219
Svyazinvest stock 12
Swift Company 215

T

TELEFAM BV 211
Telefonica de Espana SA 212
Thatcher, Margaret 30
TNK
    See: Tyumen Oil Company
Trans World Group 61, 68, 69, 72, 213
Tuapsinsky Morskoy Torgovy Port 110
Tyumen Oil Company 14, 153, 179, 206–209

U

U.S. Government's General Accounting Office 28

UNEXIM Bank 14, 15, 17, 211, 214, 215
Unified Energy Systems of Russia 101, 140, 141, 154, 179, 193, 202
United States 59, 61, 62, 138, 144, 216
Uralmash 25
Urals 140

V

Vassiliyev, Sergey 28
Vassilyev, Dmitry 28, 72
VIF
    See: Voucher Investment Funds
VNK
    See: Vostochnaya Oil Company
Volgograd 140
Vostochnaya Oil Company 14, 15, 17, 141, 153, 179
Voucher Investment Funds 57, 58, 92

Y

Yabloko, party 134, 204
Yakovlev, Vladimir 34
Yaroslavl 59
Yavlinsky, Grigory 134
Yekaterinburg 61, 115
Yeltsin, Boris 15, 19, 20, 27, 45, 73, 78, 90, 101, 104, 115, 116, 156, 158, 202, 209, 216
YUKOS 15, 101, 110, 113, 114, 118, 119, 123–125, 127, 191
YUKSI 15

Z

Zadornov, Mikhail 151
Zalogbank 67, 68, 72
Zhirinovsky, Vladimir 90
Zubov, Valery 70, 115
Zyuganov, Gennady 15, 134, 156, 158, 232